T0267294

DECISIONS OF THE
GALVESTON CAMPAIGNS

OTHER BOOKS IN THE COMMAND DECISIONS IN AMERICA'S CIVIL WAR SERIES

DECISIONS
OF THE
GALVESTON CAMPAIGNS

The Twenty-One Critical Decisions
That Defined the Operations

Edward T. Cotham Jr.

Maps by Alex Mendoza

COMMAND DECISIONS
IN AMERICA'S CIVIL WAR
Matt Spruill and Larry Peterson,
Series Editors

The University of Tennessee Press / Knoxville

Copyright © 2024 by The University of Tennessee Press / Knoxville.
All Rights Reserved. Manufactured in the United States of America.
First Edition.

Library of Congress Cataloging-in-Publication Data

Names: Cotham, Edward T. (Edward Terrel), 1953- author.
Title: Decisions of the Galveston campaigns : the twenty-one critical decisions that
defined the operations / Edward T. Cotham Jr. ; maps by Alex Mendoza.
Other titles: Command decisions in America's Civil War.
Description: First edition. | Knoxville : University of Tennessee Press, [2024] | Series:
Command decisions in America's Civil War | Includes bibliographical references and
index. | Summary: "The Galveston Campaign was a series of naval and overland bat-
tles that pitted Confederate general John B. Magruder and Texas Marine commander
Leon Smith against the armies of Isaac S. Burrell and naval forces under the command of William B. Renshaw. A Federal fleet of six ships assaulted the city on October 4, 1862, and the city surrendered after a four-day truce was agreed upon. However,
by New Year's Day of 1863, Confederate artillery reinforcements had arrived, and
Magruder coordinated a bold new attack and naval ruse with two Confederate gunboats to retake Galveston. The city would remain in the South's hands until the end of
the war and was one of the few open Confederate ports"—Provided by publisher.
Identifiers: LCCN 2024029668 | ISBN 9781621909132 (paperback) | ISBN
9781621909156 (Adobe PDF) | ISBN 9781621909149 (Kindle edition)
Subjects: LCSH: Galveston, Battle of, Galveston, Tex., 1863—Decision making. |
Sabine Pass, Battle of, Tex., 1863—Decision making. | Galveston (Tex.)—History,
Naval—19th century. | Galveston (Tex.)—History, Military--19th century. |
Texas—History—Civil War, 1861-1865.
Classification: LCC E474.1 .C673 2024 | DDC 973.7/33—dc23/eng/20240819
LC record available at https://lccn.loc.gov/2024029668

CONTENTS

ILLUSTRATIONS

Photographs

Maps

PREFACE

My interest in the campaigns directed at Galveston originated more than forty years ago, when I first wondered how and why that Texas city had achieved the distinction of being the last major Confederate port. In preparation for publishing a book about that subject in 1998, I began leading tours of Texas battlefields. I suspect that as of this writing, I may have given more tours of Civil War battlefields in Texas than anyone. As I tell tour groups, the campaigns and battles in Texas are unique and unlike those that took place in any other state. They took place on ships and on shore, during the day and at night, and lasted for periods of less than fifteen minutes to sieges that consumed multiple days of fighting. Jefferson Davis called one of the battles the most amazing victory in military history, while Adm. David Farragut called another the most embarrassing incident in the history of the US Navy. It can be debated how much the campaigns in Texas affected the wider course of the Civil War, but it has been my experience that anyone who studies the Civil War events in Texas finds them to be both unusual and remarkable.

Julius Caesar famously observed "The die is cast" after crossing the Rubicon River and precipitating a Roman civil war, but the results of decisions in the context of a military campaign are rarely that direct and foreseeable. In fact, commanders often do not even know when they are making important decisions. Perhaps that is why second-guessing commanders is one of the features that makes military history so interesting. It also makes the study of military history sometimes a more practical exercise. Over the years, I have occasionally given battlefield tours to young army officers on "staff rides," where guides like me are encouraged to put the officers in hypothetical positions, then require them to evaluate the situation and explain how they would make key decisions under those circumstances. I would usually say something like "Imagine you are officer X at this location, and these are your options. What would you choose to do?" After seeing the results of exercises like this, I now do something similar on virtually every battlefield tour I conduct. I have learned that thinking about making decisions in a "you are there" context is a useful exercise, because it forces a student to think of history in a way that gives it both a deeper meaning and more personal relevance.

As I have grown familiar with the events that took place in Civil War Texas, I have become increasingly interested in the decisions that led to them. What decisions were important and when were they made? Why did commanders make the choices they did and not make other ones? What might have happened if different decisions had been made? It became apparent to me that although I knew a great deal about what had happened, I had not given sufficient attention to the issue of just how and why events unfolded as they did. This book will isolate and address the critical decisions of the Galveston Campaigns in a focused and intensive manner. I do not exaggerate when I say that this exercise is as much for the benefit of the author as for the reader.

Like other books in the Command Decisions in America's Civil War series, this work makes use of critical-decision methodology. This approach is designed to allow someone who has an understanding of "what happened" to move to the next level and ask, "Why did it happen, or what caused it to happen?" When properly employed, the critical-decision framework is a formal construct that can be usefully applied to better understand the causes and effects that lie, usually underexplored, beneath the surface of any battle or campaign in any war.

Although the military events affecting Galveston are quite unusual, the campaigns and battles that left Galveston in Confederate hands at the end of the Civil War did not result purely from random chance. Events occurred as they did in large part because of decisions made at all levels of command on both sides. Sometimes these decisions were made months or even years before the campaigns and battles they influenced. Sometimes the decision-makers had no idea their choices would—or even could—have important consequences. In part, this is due to the difficulty of making wartime decisions.

Decisions are made constantly on the basis of limited information during the normal course of a campaign or battle. The critical-decisions methodology involves sorting through all of these determinations to determine their relative importance. As it turns out, only a small portion of them are truly important. But even seemingly important decisions can still turn out not to have much consequence to the long-term course of battle. Thus, at the top of the decision hierarchy are a select number of decisions that shape in a fundamental manner the way campaigns and battles unfold. In modern parlance, these decisions might be called "game-changers." These decisions, the basis for this book, are referred to as the "critical decisions."

Critical decisions cover the entire spectrum of war: strategy, operations, tactics, organization, personnel, and logistics. They are not always easy to identify. Initially, some decisions may appear to be minor, but actually turn out to be critical decisions that have a major impact on later events. It is also the case that a commander may perceive a decision as important that later turns out to have little or no impact on the course of a battle. It is only long after the battles and campaigns are concluded, with the advantage of time and hindsight, that historians can look back and determine which decisions were critical and analyze how they were made. That study, finding and exploring the "critical decisions" of the Galveston Campaigns, is what this book is all about.

It is important that the reader understands this concept of a critical decision. Without this comprehension, a book such as this may appear to be only a short and selective narrative history of the Civil War in Texas. This is not that sort of history. Instead, it is a study in command that is intended to explore how the Galveston engagements unfolded as they did; it is about the "why" instead of the "what happened."

To better illustrate the concepts discussed before, this chart shows the decisions hierarchy pyramid. At the bottom are all the decisions in a battle or campaign. Above those are a lesser number of important decisions, and at the top are the very small number of critical decisions.

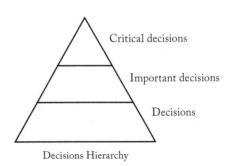

Decisions Hierarchy

This book is all about the decisions at the top of that pyramid. How do they reach the top of the pyramid and warrant inclusion in this book? The criterion for a critical decision is that it is of such magnitude that it shaped not only the events immediately following, but also the campaigns or battles from that point on. If these choices had not been made, or if different ones had been made, the sequence of events for the Galveston Campaigns and battles would likely have been significantly different.

The critical decisions featured in this book were chosen based on my decades of experience leading Texas battlefield tours and a close reading and research of primary and secondary source material. Other historians might choose different decisions or interpret critical events in a different manner. However, the critical decisions enumerated in this book are what I believe to be the most important and impactful ones of the campaigns and battles that affected Galveston. Had they been made otherwise, the character of the campaigns, the battles, and the decisions that followed would have been different. These differences would have been of such magnitude as to change the sequence of events from that point on.

This is not to say that if critical decisions had been made differently, Union forces would have controlled Texas and Galveston from the fall of 1862 until the end of the war, although events might well have turned out that way. That is beyond the scope of this book. It is enough to say that if the critical decisions had been altered, subsequent events would have been significantly different, and the outcome might well have changed. The sequence of events leading to an outcome would certainly have been different, and the orientation of the opposing forces would probably have been different. In addition, the way forces collided might have had a completely different trajectory and occurred at different times or places.

This is not a history of the Civil War in Texas, nor is it a history of the various battles involving Galveston. Instead, this book focuses on the critical decisions that affected the way both those events turned out. It will lay out some basic facts concerning the available options and decisions, and then use that information to present what is hopefully a relatively clear outline of some very complex situations. Without neglecting important details, this account is designed to present the reader with a coherent and manageable blueprint to determine why the key campaigns and battles in Texas turned out as they did.

The decisions are grouped into specific time periods. Within these time periods each critical decision is presented and discussed in detail, generally in the following format: the situation, options (courses of action) available to the decision-maker, the decision that was made, the results/outcome of that decision, and, in some cases, other possible outcomes had another option been chosen.

It should be acknowledged at the outset that many of the critical decisions had results that differed from those the decision-maker anticipated. Events were frequently influenced, sometimes greatly, by chance or luck. These unpredictable factors can make what initially appear to be good decisions, under the right conditions, produce adverse results. Likewise, what initially appear as bad decisions can sometimes produce positive results. For this reason, I will generally refrain from characterizing a decision as good or bad. Instead, the narrative that follows concentrates on the actual consequences or results of each decision and enables the reader to see how that decision affected subsequent campaigns or battles.

There is value in being in proximity to the ground where a decision was made or carried out. Indeed, that is the reason that I am such a great proponent of in-person battlefield tours. Being on the ground, even in an urban setting like Galveston, provides an interested observer with the opportunity to view the terrain and the tactical situation as the decision-makers did. This can be difficult in Texas because of the absence of any preserved Civil War battlefields maintained by an entity like the National Park Service. However, the Sabine Pass Battleground State Historic Site is an excellent state park, and some of the critical decisions discussed in this book were made and carried out at or near the Galveston or Sabine Pass battlefields. For this reason, this work includes an appendix with a guided tour of some of the key battlefields involved in the Galveston Campaigns. My hope is that this book with its battlefield guide appendix will form a foundation for those wishing to conduct further reading, study, and reflection on the Galveston Campaigns and the battles and skirmishes that occurred throughout.

I wish to acknowledge and thank the many who assisted me in researching and writing this book. I particularly want to thank Matt Spruill and Larry Peterson, who served as my constant guides in adapting the history of the Texas Campaigns to the critical-decision format that they helped develop. I also want to thank my friend Donald S. Frazier, who has been my constant guide in researching and writing about the military aspects of Texas history since his *Cottonclads!* was published in 1996. Finally, I want to thank my many friends at the Galveston Historical Foundation and the Rosenberg Library, who have continually supported my historical journey over the course of many years. And now on to the critical decisions. As I say to all my readers and students, "See you on the battlefield!"

INTRODUCTION

The first full year of the Civil War, 1862, saw both sides taking bold risks with but little to show in the way of results. The year began with Texas forces under the command of Brig. Gen. Henry Hopkins Sibley making a strong move into New Mexico in an attempt to expand Confederate territories toward the Pacific coast. Although initially successful, this campaign failed to gain any serious traction, and by summer what was left of the heavily depleted force barely managed to straggle back to Texas. Some of these troops would later play a major role in the Confederate recapture of Galveston.[1]

Earlier in the Civil War, Gen. Braxton Bragg had turned down the chance to command the Confederate department that included Texas. It was a decision that he might later have regretted. In the late summer of 1862, Bragg led his Army of the Mississippi into Kentucky. Although his position on the Ohio River had clear strategic value, he failed to achieve his objectives at the Battle of Perryville on October 8, 1862, and was forced to retreat into Tennessee. As the Confederates were recapturing Galveston on January 1, 1863, Bragg was in the process of fighting (and losing) the Battle of Stones River near Murfreesboro, Tennessee. Bragg served as a railroad engineer in Galveston after the war and died there in 1876.[2]

In March 1862, Maj. Gen. George McClellan landed a huge Union army on the peninsula leading up to Richmond, Virginia, and began a slow advance toward the Confederate capital. From June 25 to July 1, 1862, Robert E. Lee's Army of Northern Virginia fought a series of desperate battles known as the

Seven Days' Campaign. Featuring a general (John Bankhead Magruder) who would later play the starring role in the Battle of Galveston, Lee's army drove McClellan's army back from the gates of Richmond. A few months later, Lee followed up his success by crossing his army over the Potomac River into Maryland. On September 17, 1862, Lee and McClellan squared off again at the Battle of Antietam, the deadliest one-day battle in American history. A tactical draw, the fighting resulted in Lee's retreat from Maryland.[3]

By the summer of 1862, Vicksburg was the most important Confederate stronghold on the Mississippi River. The Union navy attempted to capture it in May but was unsuccessful. Maj. Gen. Ulysses S. Grant started a promising campaign in November 1862 that involved splitting his army in half and coming at the city from two separate directions. Grant's wing was stopped when a Confederate raid on Holly Springs destroyed his main supply depot. A second wing under the command of Maj. Gen. William T. Sherman made a landing on the Yazoo River and approached Vicksburg from the north. Between December 26 and 29, 1862, Sherman's force was turned back at the Battle of Chickasaw Bayou. As events later played out, Grant would not capture Vicksburg until July 4, 1863. An elated President Lincoln greeted Grant's momentous achievement by noting, "The Father of Waters again goes unvexed to the sea."[4]

Just as Union and Confederate military planners viewed Vicksburg as the key to controlling the Mississippi River, both sides saw Galveston, Texas, as the key to controlling the vast area west of the Mississippi. The reason for this prominence had to do with geography. Although the Department of the Trans-Mississippi that the Confederacy designated in 1862 included Texas, Arkansas, Missouri, west Louisiana, and the Indian Territory, only Texas had a material coastline that would support external trade. In fact, the Texas coast extended for almost four hundred miles, making it one of the longest and most accessible coastlines in the entire South.[5]

In addition, Texas possessed something relatively rare: a port that could accommodate oceangoing vessels. That port was Galveston, the state's largest city in 1861. The "Island City," as Galveston was known, featured what one historian has accurately called the "finest harbor on the entire Gulf of Mexico."[6]

What made Galveston unique as a port was the depth of water leading into Galveston Bay. When Abraham Lincoln proclaimed a blockade of Southern ports in 1861, the navy's Blockade Strategy Board prioritized obstructing those that could accommodate vessels with a draft (depth from the waterline to the keel) of twelve feet. Among Texas ports, only Galveston met the twelve-foot requirement. The board described Galveston as "the analogue of Charleston in its depth of water" and advised, "[An] efficient blockade of Galveston is, in fact, the blockade of the coast of Texas."[7]

Modern photograph of large ship traffic at the entrance to Galveston Bay. Author's collection.

As the blockade board could plainly see, there was no mystery why Galveston needed to be blockaded. On the eve of the Civil War, the city was one of the fastest growing ports in the nation. Of the 300,000 bales of cotton exported from Texas in 1860, 200,000 were compressed and loaded on board vessels at Galveston. A British consular official estimated that in 1861 prior to the war, Galveston was positioned to easily expand that number to 400,000, with millions more bales of potential exports on the horizon. Not all of the export business involved cotton; other items loaded onto ships included corn, sugar, deerskins, hides, cottonseed, and tobacco.[8] The 1861 *Texas Almanac* reported that the value of exports from Galveston between 1858 and 1861 had been growing at the rate of almost 50 percent per year. "The steady increase

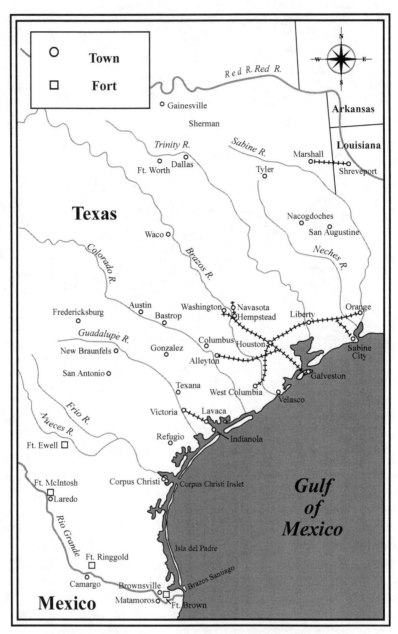

Map of the Texas Coast Showing Key Cities (1861–1865)

in the trade and general business of Galveston," the editors boasted, "leaves no room to doubt that it must ere long rival many of the principal seaports of the South."[9]

Not only was Galveston the best port on the Gulf Coast, it was also the terminus for the railroad system of Texas, which extended north to the Houston area and then spread out like the fingers of a hand. Although important to the rapidly expanding Texas export economy, the Texas railroad network had important limitations as the Civil War approached. To begin with, it did not connect to any of the other national railroad systems, extending only to a point near the Louisiana border on the east. Equally problematic was the fact that the railroads had a number of different gauges, making it difficult to transfer any cargo a long distance on a single car. Because of these limitations, the commercial traffic converging at Galveston was carried by both railcars and packet steamboats. One of the geographic advantages of Galveston Bay was that emptying into it were the Trinity River, which was navigable to destinations in east Texas, and Buffalo Bayou, which extended northwest to Houston.[10]

The fact that Galveston was on an island gave it certain commercial advantages, but it also meant that a bridge would be needed if trains were to reach the port. On February 6, 1860, the Galveston, Houston and Henderson Railroad created the first trestle, extending approximately two miles from Virginia Point on the mainland to Galveston Island. This was built as a dedicated railroad bridge, and any use of it as a conventional road system would require planking over it. As military planners later found out, planking the bridge was not impossible, but it would take time and disrupt rail traffic.

Although Galveston was the primary Texas port, Houston was the central hub for Texas railroads. Crops and products from across Texas were typically gathered in the Houston area and then forwarded to Galveston by rail or steamboat. It only took a brief glance at a map to realize that Galveston and Houston were the primary axes of the Texas economy. In fact, it is not going too far to say that at the time of the Civil War, Galveston and Houston were the keys to Texas.[11]

The blockade of Texas was initiated on the afternoon of July 2, 1861, when the Union steamer *South Carolina* appeared off the entrance to Galveston Bay. A month later, a small, indecisive engagement took place between the Union vessel and a Confederate battery on the beach. The rest of 1861 proceeded with relatively little action between the blockaders and the blockaded city. As the beginning of 1862 approached, a crucial question still had not been answered: Were the Confederates committed and able to defend Galveston Island? The answer to this question would be the first critical decision involving the Galveston Campaigns.

CHAPTER 1

DEFENDING AN ISLAND

There were several interesting personalities initially chosen to command the defenses of Galveston. A "Committee on Public Safety" first put Gen. Sidney Sherman in charge. Sherman, whose claim to fame was that he had led the charge of the left wing of the Texian Army at the Battle of San Jacinto, realized immediately that he did not have the resources to do the job. He had few pieces of artillery and was disgusted to learn that he had insufficient ammunition even to fire those he possessed.[1]

The first formally appointed commander of the Confederate defenses of Texas was Col. (later Gen.) Earl Van Dorn, who arrived at Galveston in April 1861. Van Dorn quickly made a name for himself, capturing the *Star of the West* in Matagorda Bay and forcing the surrender of six companies of US infantry at Saluria. Confederate officials in Richmond soon saw that Van Dorn was destined for higher command. In August 1861, he was promoted and summoned to the Confederate capital.[2] By this time Sidney Sherman had resigned, angrily telling his men that his lack of authority as Galveston's commander was a constant source of embarrassment.[3]

The man who eventually replaced Van Dorn in command of the Texas defenses was a dramatic change from the men who had preceded him. Brig. Gen. Paul Octave Hébert grew up in a wealthy Louisiana family and had all the advantages that position offered. He graduated first in the 1840 class at West Point and served with distinction in the Mexican War. In fact, dispatches referred to him as "the gallant young Creole colonel." After the Mexican War,

Brig. Gen. Paul Octave Hébert, CSA.
LC Control No. 2002711379. Library of
Congress.

Hébert was elected the youngest governor of Louisiana. When the Civil War broke out, he was commissioned as a colonel in the First Louisiana Artillery but was soon promoted to brigadier general. In August 1861, Hébert was transferred to Texas to replace Van Dorn. He made his way to Galveston, and quickly realized that his first strategic challenge involved deciding whether to defend the island.[4]

Hébert Decides Not to Oppose Union Efforts to Capture Galveston Island

Situation

General Hébert arrived in Galveston to find the defensive effort in chaos. On September 27, 1861, he reported to Secretary of War Judah P. Benjamin in Richmond:

> I find this coast in almost a defenseless state, and in the total want of proper works and armaments; the task of defending successfully any point against an attack of any magnitude amounts to a military impossibility. The port of Galveston is partially defended by a few open sand works, mounted with guns of calibers ranging from 18-pounders

to 32-pounders, and of course totally inadequate to resist a
bombardment with heavy guns. The few large guns now
on the way, should they not arrive too late, will in some
measure increase the efficiency of the harbor defenses. On
a coast like this, however, where in calm weather a landing
can be effected at any point, and the bays in the rear and
flank of Galveston Island reached in that manner or by the
pass at the west end, the problem of defense, considering
the means available to that effect, is certainly one of very
difficult, if not impossible, solution.[5]

It is easy to understand why General Hébert saw the defense of Galveston Island as such a formidable challenge. At West Point, the general would undoubtedly have studied the campaigns of the American Revolution and learned the difficulty that George Washington had encountered in defending the island of Manhattan against the British, leading him ultimately to abandon it and retreat to New Jersey. There was just no getting around the fact that islands posed military problems. The Civil War had started with the unsuccessful defense of an island fortification at Fort Sumter, and several island forts had subsequently fallen to attacking forces.

Islands are by definition subject to encirclement, and a city located on an island must be prepared to defend itself against a potential attack from any and all directions. Galveston Island was approximately twenty-seven miles long and no more than three miles wide at its widest point. The city of Galveston was located near the eastern tip of the island. The western portion of Galveston Island was relatively uninhabited, and it didn't take much imagination to envision a sudden landing near the western end of the island, followed by a rapid march against what was in 1861 a largely unfortified city.

Another factor that undoubtedly worried Hébert was the nature of the potential attacking force. By the time of his arrival in Galveston, several Union warships were already blockading the entrance to the bay, and there were rumors that a large Union fleet carrying an invading army was already on its way to the Gulf. For all Hébert knew, the US Navy might sail boldly into Galveston Harbor one morning, cut off his route of retreat to the mainland, and then bombard his position into submission from long range.

Hébert warned Secretary Benjamin that his island command might end up being another case like Fort Hatteras, where Union gunboats had simply launched a bombardment so severe that it forced the entire garrison to surrender.[6] Hébert's fears about the threat posed by Union naval forces seemed confirmed when a daring nighttime raid entered Galveston Bay on November 7, captured the small Confederate schooner *Royal Yacht's* crew, and left the schooner on fire. If he could not even protect his few vessels against small boat attacks, how could he hope to defend an entire island?[7]

Hébert had no significant naval assets of his own and knew that he lacked the expertise to manage such assets even if they were available. He was an engineer and a politician, not a sailor. Nothing in his experience in the Mexican War had prepared him to mount a significant defense against Union gunboats. He confessed to Secretary Benjamin that he could see all the problems but none of the solutions. "I much fear," he admitted, "that I have brought my little military reputation to an early grave."[8] As he studied his limited options for the defense of Galveston, Hébert knew that he had a difficult decision to make.

Options

Hébert had three options. He could stay and defend the island, or he could abandon Galveston to the enemy. He could also make a show of defending the island until the enemy showed up in force, and then evacuate the island.

Option 1

Hébert could stay and fight. He could continue to build up the defenses of Galveston Island, fortify the area around the port and city as best he could, and then hope that more guns and defenders eventually arrived before a powerful Union fleet did. Choosing to stay and fight had the advantage of popularity with Texans (particularly Galvestonians) and their public officials. If he could successfully defend Galveston, it would also add to Hébert's reputation. But it represented a serious gamble.

A week following the *Royal Yacht* incident, Hébert wrote once again to Secretary Benjamin, noting that there was no getting around one fact: "This city is on an island, connected with the mainland by only one railroad bridge." As far as Hébert could tell, the defense of Galveston in the event of a formidable attack was a "very difficult if not an impossible matter." To Hébert, "prudence would dictate that all proper precautions should be taken to get the troops off in the event of a necessity of abandoning or being driven from the island."[9]

Option 2

Hébert seriously considered the immediate evacuation of Galveston Island. If he moved now, he could take his time and fortify a more defensible position on the mainland near the railroad connection to Houston. This would eliminate the threat of being surrounded by gunboats and enable Hébert to defend the main approaches to Houston and its critical railroad network. Preserving his small force's ability to continue the fight might be vital when a sizable Union force eventually arrived to launch a major invasion of Texas.

The disadvantage of this course of action was that it essentially abandoned what was then the largest and most important Texas city without a fight. No matter its strategic merits, this decision would be perceived in an extremely negative light by Texans, many of whom had property or business interests in the Galveston area, and had family members fighting elsewhere in the Confederate armies. Texas was a state with its historic roots in battles like the Alamo. Running away from a fight was not something to which Texans were accustomed. It would be particularly distasteful if the decision to evacuate Galveston, the state's key city, was announced by a Louisiana general. As a politician, Hébert knew that any choice he made to surrender Galveston would be received very badly by the Texans he was supposedly tasked to defend.

Option 3

Hébert's third option was to gradually retreat from Galveston Island without making any public announcement that he intended to do so. If he slowly moved supplies and guns to the mainland, maybe nobody would notice. He could build a major fortification at Virginia Point, where the railroad bridge contacted the mainland, and then retreat to this prepared position when the enemy eventually appeared in force. If he could maintain the illusion of defending Galveston long enough, Hébert might deter the enemy from advancing and taking the city for an extended period. This plan would not keep Galveston in Confederate hands when the challenge inevitably came, but it would at least postpone Union possession of the city and its port for a time.

This option would require Hébert to leave many of his troops and some of his guns on the island until the last possible minute. The risk of this plan was that the timing was very tricky. A large Union force might suddenly appear and rapidly occupy Galveston Island, preventing the Confederates from retreating with all their remaining guns and military supplies. If the enemy caught the Confederates with half their forces on the island and half on the mainland, this option might result in disaster. Leaving suddenly when the enemy appeared might also endanger the civilians who continued living in the city and depended on the army for protection.

Decision

Hébert decided to evacuate the island while maintaining the pretense that he would defend it. Although he continued to believe that defending Galveston from a serious attack was impossible, Hébert told Secretary Benjamin that honor required that "an effort must be made in that direction, and this place held as long as possible."[10]

Results/Impact

Hébert's decision meant that Galveston would stay in Confederate hands until a Union fleet arrived in the fall of 1862. If he had allowed the enemy to take control of the island at an earlier time, it is possible, even likely, that a large occupying force would have been sent by the Union much sooner. This might well have prevented the Confederates from successfully recapturing Galveston as they eventually did at the beginning of 1863. Hébert's decision to move most of the artillery pieces to the mainland also kept them out of Union hands when the city was eventually captured in 1862. More importantly, it left these guns conveniently positioned to be moved to the island and used by Confederate forces during the Battle of Galveston. Although Hébert's choice to not defend the island was severely criticized by Texans in 1862, it ended up helping—perhaps unintentionally—to set the stage for Confederate success in 1863.

Hébert's gamble that he could wait and still evacuate the bulk of his forces almost failed. There was a brief scare in May 1862 when Capt. Henry Eagle of the blockading squadron made a bold demand for Galveston's surrender. But General Hébert correctly sensed that, on this occasion, the ultimatum was a bluff. He did not put his full-scale emergency evacuation plan into effect. Instead, he directed his subordinates merely to respond that Eagle would receive an answer if and only if a substantial Union force materialized to back up his demand.[11]

While waiting for the many Federals he expected to arrive, Hébert ordered the construction of a major fortification on the mainland, ironically named Fort Hébert in his honor. This bastion had the railroad from Galveston to Houston passing through its middle. He then planned to begin planking over the railroad bridge to give the Confederates a good opportunity to evacuate the island with most of their guns when the time came. He instructed his artillery batteries at the entrance to Galveston Bay that in the event a large Union naval force appeared, they were to fire their guns once, then spike their batteries and evacuate to the fortifications on the mainland.

Although Hébert publicly proclaimed that he intended to defend Galveston, it became clear to civilians in the area that he had ordered the Confederates to gradually move their best armament to the mainland and deplete the defenses on the island. Rumors that Galveston was in the process of being evacuated were everywhere. In Austin, Texas governor Francis R. Lubbock was alarmed by these reports and warned Hébert that if Galveston was given

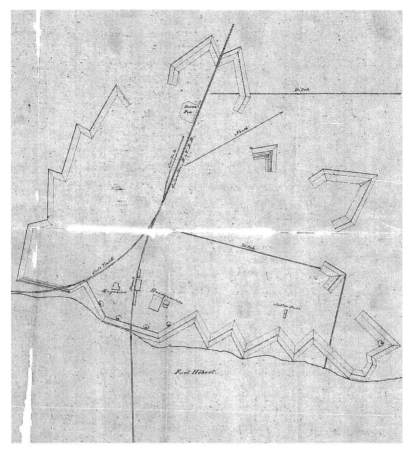

Map of Fort Hébert, Virginia Point, Texas, circa 1862. Image 1195.1B.
Rosenberg Library, Galveston, Texas.

over to the enemy without a spirited fight, "it would dispirit the people from
one end of the State to the other."[12]

The people of Galveston were not fooled; they could see the steady stream
of portable property, public and private, departing the island. Not all of the
transferred items stayed at Fort Hébert. The hospital stores, along with the
Galveston newspaper, were moved to Houston. "Demoralization grew apace,"
Lubbock wrote, noting that the people of Texas came to realize that Hébert
was "bewildered at the magnitude of the task assigned him" and lacked any
coherent plan to defend them. Even though Galveston had not yet fallen,
Texans knew that it was only a matter of time. Their morale simply collapsed.

While Texas civilians' sons and husbands were off fighting Union armies, Confederate officials in the state seemed to lack the will even to attempt to fight for their homes.[13]

Hébert's choice to gradually bleed Galveston of its defenses made him extremely unpopular with Texans. As Thomas North wrote, "Everybody became tired and disgusted with the General and his policy." Not only were Hébert's policies distasteful, but he dressed in ways that did not suit "the ideas and ways of a pioneer country." Even worse, "he was suspected of cowardice."[14]

The final card was played on October 4, 1862, when Cmdre. William B. Renshaw entered Galveston Bay with a fleet of Union gunboats and called for the city's surrender. Nothing about this demand was subtle. As Hébert later reported, Renshaw warned that "he would hoist the United States flag over the city of Galveston or its ashes."[15]

Consistent with Hébert's contingency plan, the Confederates at Fort Point near the entrance to the bay fired their gun at the Union fleet once, spiked it, and then began their planned movement off the island with everything they could carry. This could have been a disaster for Hébert if the Union gunboats had suddenly bombarded the city or immediately attempted to destroy the railroad bridge. But instead of launching any immediate attack, Renshaw agreed to a four-day truce period to allow civilians to evacuate the city.

This truce was a strategic error on Renshaw's part. The Confederates used this unexpected grace period, later the subject of controversy, to withdraw their remaining forces, all of the machinery, and at least four large guns to Virginia Point. After the expiration of the cease-fire, the only Confederate stronghold left on Galveston Island was a small fort at Eagle Grove near the entrance to the railroad bridge. At Virginia Point the Confederates completed their long-planned movement into Fort Hébert. Because of its strategic position guarding the railroad line across from Galveston, Fort Hébert would end up being one of the largest continuously occupied fortified positions in Civil War Texas. If it were up to General Hébert, however, the Confederates would not have stayed there very long. Even as his forces moved in, the general was already making contingency plans to relocate even farther into the interior, with his next planned stop almost fifty miles away near Houston.[16]

Because of Hébert's evacuation decision, neither the Union nor the Confederate forces suffered a single casualty in the capture of Galveston. Instead, after the expiration of the four-day truce period, Union naval forces calmly entered the city and raised the US flag over the customhouse. A young Union marine from Pennsylvania called this ceremony a "gala occasion" and described the people of Galveston who witnessed it as the most "respectable and well-behaved set" he had ever seen.[17]

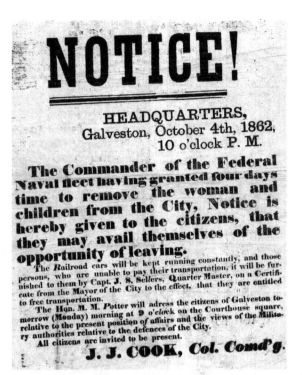

Evacuation notice dated October 4, 1862, issued by Col. Joseph J. Cook, CSA. Rosenberg Library, Galveston, Texas.

The capture of Galveston occurred so smoothly and easily that Union commanders were given a false impression about Texans' ability and willingness to fight. Adm. David G. Farragut later sent Renshaw a letter congratulating him on the "easy conquest" he had made of the city. He then forwarded Renshaw's report to Secretary of the Navy Gideon Welles, together with a request for soldiers to garrison Galveston and a few other places that had been seized on the Texas coast. "All we want," Farragut boasted, "is a few soldiers to hold the places and we will soon have the whole coast."[18]

Farragut did not know it, but even as he wrote his boasting message to Washington, General Hébert's time in Texas was coming to an end. A new Confederate commander would soon be arriving from Virginia. That bold and dashing officer was on the opposite end of the aggressiveness spectrum from Hébert. He would make different decisions regarding the strategic importance of Galveston, with very different results.

CHAPTER 2

THE CONFEDERATE RECAPTURE
OF GALVESTON

From its capture by the Union navy in October 1862 until the beginning of 1863, the city of Galveston remained under the guns of a naval force in Galveston Harbor. The lack of a significant Union infantry presence, however, meant that Confederate scouts and spies were able to continue to maintain a significant presence in the city, particularly at night when the Union marines retreated to their ships. With Federals controlling the harbor and Confederates having at least partial control of the city, it was clear to both sides that this tense and unstable standoff was unlikely to endure very long. Newspapers in Texas ominously predicted that Union military planners would soon send a large force of infantry to use Galveston as the launching point for an invasion of Texas. Over in New Orleans, Admiral Farragut was indeed pressing the army to send reinforcements and demanding that Texas be invaded as soon as possible. President Lincoln himself was said to favor sending a strong force to the state.

The only thing that might potentially derail the invasion of Texas would be a quick Confederate recapture of Galveston. Although such a result seemed highly unlikely as the New Year of 1863 approached, a plan was indeed underway to attempt to accomplish that result. Ten critical decisions led to what became known as the Battle of Galveston, and to Confederate success at that engagement.

Jefferson Davis Sends Magruder to Texas

Situation

Probably the most impactful decision for the Texas Campaigns was made by a political figure outside the state, and it involved an officer who was not within a thousand miles of Galveston Island when it was abandoned to the Union in the fall of 1862. The political figure who made the decision was Confederate president Jefferson Davis, and the decision involved the fate of Maj. Gen. John Bankhead Magruder. Magruder was a Virginian who had graduated in the West Point class of 1830 (one class after Robert E. Lee and two classes after Jefferson Davis).

Because of his long tenure with the army, Magruder and his eccentricities were well known to all the major military figures in the Civil War. Unusual for a military school graduate, Magruder exhibited a particular talent for theater. In Texas before the outset of the Mexican War, he staged a production in camp of Shakespeare's *Othello* that was at one point intended to feature future generals James Longstreet and U. S. Grant. Once the Mexican War started in earnest, Magruder performed well, successfully leading an artillery

Maj. Gen. John Bankhead
Magruder, CSA. Name File—
Photograph Collection. Rosenberg
Library, Galveston, Texas.

force that included future Confederate legend Thomas J. "Stonewall" Jackson. Magruder was popular with the officers of the antebellum army, who gave him the nickname "Prince John" because of his flamboyant mannerisms and eccentric behavior. Despite his popularity and demonstrated military prowess, there was one clear warning sign in the Virginian's early career. Magruder developed a well-deserved reputation for partying and drinking to excess, and when the Civil War began in 1861, there were some in the new Confederate army who feared giving him any substantial command.[1]

Magruder's early Civil War experience was confined to Virginia. In 1861, he was placed in charge of the defenses of the peninsula that led to Richmond. This type of assignment was perfect for his talents. When Maj. Gen. George McClellan led an immense Union army toward the Confederate capital in the spring of 1862, Magruder performed brilliantly at first, devising a whole series of diversions and illusions to keep McClellan from advancing. His men marched back and forth in spread-out formations and lit additional campfires at night to disguise their true numbers. McClellan and his spies were deceived by Magruder's clever schemes and delayed hurling their forces against Richmond's relatively weak defenses.

When it eventually became necessary for the Confederates to act, new commander of the army Robert E. Lee made the bold decision to divide his numerically smaller army and move the bulk of it north of the Chickahominy River, where it could launch a surprise attack against the flank of a smaller, isolated Federal force. It was a remarkable and risky gamble. Lee's plan left only two divisions, about twenty-five thousand men, between McClellan's force of more than sixty-five thousand men and Richmond. Magruder, who commanded one of those two divisions, would have to put on the performance of his life to convince McClellan to stay in place and maintain only a defensive posture. He proved up for the occasion, ordering simulated preparations for attack with blowing bugles and short artillery bombardments. Magruder's plan worked. Gen. D. H. Hill later called him "the master of ruses and strategy" for the creative and effective demonstrations that kept the Union forces immobilized.[2]

When Lee's plan succeeded and the Union army began to retreat, Lee ordered Magruder to leave his defensive position and pursue the enemy. Lee hoped to fix McClellan in place and possibly bring on a decisive engagement. It is at this point that an exhausted Magruder turned cautious and began to underperform Lee's expectations. After the Battle of Savage's Station on June 29, 1862, Magruder was criticized for not pressing the attack as Lee had ordered. Three days later, he responded to Lee's pointed criticism by pressing an assault at Malvern Hill that never should have been made. Believing that he was acting as Lee had ordered, Magruder directed his men to attack into the teeth of a Union position that not only had a mass of artillery but also was supported by fire from Union gunboats to its rear. One observer accurately described the terrible result: "It was not war—it was murder."[3]

As the casualty count at Malvern Hill became public, Magruder received a great deal of criticism both in the press and in the army for his performance. Some rumors claimed he had been drunk; others said he must have ignored orders or had exhibited cowardice on the battlefield. Historians have debated the accuracy of these accusations, but there can be no dispute that Magruder did not satisfy Lee's needs and expectations in the final days of the Seven Days' Campaign. Not used to such negative attention and believing that he had performed remarkably well given the circumstances, Magruder was now eager to get away from Richmond and his persecutors. The general must have considered himself fortunate to have already received orders to go somewhere different for an independent command and a change of scenery. But this transfer turned out not to be the simple escape he assumed.[4]

Magruder had indeed received orders dated May 23, 1862, appointing him to command the District of the Trans-Mississippi, which included Texas and all of the Confederacy west of the Mississippi River. This was over a month before the Seven Days' Battles. At Magruder's request, those orders had been temporarily suspended while the campaign to defend Richmond was ongoing. After the campaign was over and the Federal army had departed, the suspension was lifted, and Magruder was once again given orders to proceed to his new command. On July 2, 1862, the general departed for his next assignment. It is at this point that the situation suddenly changed dramatically for Magruder and his military career.[5]

During the campaigns around Richmond, Robert H. Chilton served as Lee's chief of staff. A Virginian, Chilton had been serving in Texas when the war broke out. Although he was a close friend of Lee's, he was not a very competent staff officer. Chilton and the rest of the general's staff performed very poorly during the actions around Richmond. The orders that Chilton drafted during the Seven Days battles were at best confusing and sometimes contradictory. An argument can be easily made that his sloppy orders to Magruder were a central cause of the debacle at Malvern Hill. Perhaps because he was looking for a scapegoat, Chilton decided that the time was ripe to blame Magruder for a major part of the failure to capture McClellan's army.[6]

On July 11, 1862, Chilton wrote to Inspector General Samuel Cooper, urging him to rescind Magruder's assignment to command in the Trans-Mississippi. Saying that Magruder was "incompetent to command," Chilton charged that it would be a "sad injustice to be inflicted upon the people of the

Jefferson Davis, president of the
Confederate States of America.
LC-USZ62-8999. Library of
Congress.

Southwest by sending someone so utterly incompetent and deficient." He said
that General Lee concurred in his belief that Magruder was unfit and that
Gen. D. R. Jones "charge[d] him with something worse than incompetency."[7]

Although this latter charge was not defined, because of Magruder's reputation it presumably involved drunkenness. Cooper, who already had a low
opinion of Magruder from experiences before the war, immediately forwarded
Chilton's letter to Jefferson Davis, along with his own observation that "the
partially reformed drunkard will as surely return to his cup as 'the dog to
his vomit.'" Faced with these serious charges, Davis recalled Magruder via
telegraph and on July 16 appointed Theophilus Holmes to command the
Trans-Mississippi. Suddenly, Magruder was in the fight of his life to preserve
his military reputation and career.[8]

Davis knew Magruder very well. Although they had not been in the same
class, both had been cadets at West Point at the same time. They had subsequently served in the Mexican War at the same time. Davis was all too
aware of Magruder's reputation for drinking. Indeed, earlier in the war, he
had requested and obtained a personal pledge of sobriety from Magruder
before promoting him. To receive these disturbing reports now, supposedly
endorsed by trustworthy people like Cooper and Lee, was deeply troubling to
Davis. It left him in a difficult position.[9]

Options

Davis had three options: He could deny Magruder any new assignment and force him to resign his command. Alternatively, he could put Magruder's fate in the hands of a court of inquiry, or he could go ahead and give Magruder an assignment in the Southwest.

Option 1

Davis could deny Magruder any new assignment. If he did this, he would essentially be ending Magruder's long military career and forcing him to resign. If the complaints about Magruder's incompetence and drinking were true, this course of action would be appropriate, if not long overdue. It would also satisfy a host of army officers and members of the press who now piled on and blamed Magruder for the debacle at Malvern Hill and the unsuccessful end of the Peninsula Campaign. On the other hand, if the complaints were false, running Magruder off would deprive the army of the services of an experienced commander who had already proved his worth at battles like Big Bethel and the skirmishing on the Virginia Peninsula before the Seven Days battles. Although Davis did not seem to care much for Magruder as a person, he knew that the general exhibited a rare talent in the Confederate army. He designed and fought battles in unconventional ways. Davis wondered whether Magruder might be better used as an independent commander, and not as a division or corps commander under someone like Lee. Texas might be the ideal place to send an unconventional leader who had shown an ability to do more with less. If Davis ended Magruder's career in scandal, he would never learn how such an experiment would play out.

Option 2

Davis could order that a court of inquiry be conducted concerning the charges leveled against Magruder. After all, stripped of their sensational elements, all Davis really had at this point were some uncorroborated complaints by a staff officer and some speculation that Magruder might have returned to old vices. Ordering a court of inquiry would have the virtue of providing a more complete record from which Davis could make a more informed decision. It would also give Magruder a fair chance to vindicate his honor. The disadvantage of a court of inquiry was that it would consume a great deal of time and resources, and occupy a number of key military officers in a process that would distract them from fighting the enemy.

<u>Option 3</u>

Davis could ignore the charges against Magruder and forward him to a command in the Southwest. There was certainly a need for experienced commanders in that perpetually neglected part of the Confederacy. The people of Texas were clamoring for a new, more aggressive leader to replace General Hébert, and Magruder appeared to fit the bill perfectly. In Texas, Davis knew, Magruder would not have to interact with Chilton, Cooper, or his other Virginia detractors. Instead, this might be just the kind of fresh start to rejuvenate a gallant officer's career and return him to public favor.

If the charges were true, however, and Chilton was right in criticizing Magruder, sending the controversial general to the Southwest might result in a new series of disasters. Davis could certainly imagine the blame that might attach to the official who sent a known drunkard he had been warned against to an important military command.

Decision

Davis decided to send Magruder to a new command in Texas. Before doing so, Davis conducted a personal interview with the general and informed him of the serious charges that had been leveled against him. Magruder responded by quickly compiling a report refuting each accusation, which he then expanded into a lengthy response that contained sworn statements from a number of witnesses. The witnesses included a surgeon who testified that he knew the signs of alcohol influence, and that Magruder had never exhibited them.[10]

Faced with Magruder's detailed response, Chilton waffled on his original allegations. Davis learned that General Jones denied Chilton's claim that he had made any charge against Magruder, and Lee, who had not been advised of Chilton's claims before they were submitted, told Davis that as far as he could determine, "General Magruder intentionally omitted nothing that he could do to insure success." It was not an unqualified endorsement, but it did suggest that Lee did not agree with Chilton's most serious charges. After reviewing the evidence, Davis swept the charges under the rug and sent Magruder on his way to Texas.[11]

Results/Impact

Magruder was delighted to receive word of his restored assignment to the Southwest. Although the general was not placed in charge of the entire Trans-Mississippi as he believed he deserved, on October 10, 1862, he was given command of the District of Texas, New Mexico, and Arizona. It was still an important post. In Texas, Magruder could finally make his own plans and see them implemented, free of the bureaucracy and politics of the army in Richmond.[12]

Sending Magruder to Texas under these conditions made an enormous difference in the way the campaigns to recapture Galveston and defend Texas played out. Without Magruder, Galveston might never have been recaptured. General Hébert, whom Magruder replaced, had surrendered the city to the Union without any serious fight. It is doubtful whether any other Confederate commander would have come to Texas so determined to immediately recapture the city, particularly with the bold and risky battle plan that soon proved successful. It is not going too far to say that no other commander in the war ever launched a comparable battle.

Because of Davis's decision, Magruder came to Texas with something to prove to his detractors. Although it would not be easy, he was absolutely determined to make a name for himself by recapturing Galveston. His positive attitude was just what Texans wanted. Col. John S. "RIP" Ford wrote that the "advent of General Magruder was equal to the addition of 50,000 men to the forces of Texas." According to Ford, Magruder's motto was "'Ready."[13] Davis did not know it when he transferred Magruder to Texas, but he had found exactly the right man at the right time for an incredibly difficult job.

Magruder Determines That Galveston Has to Be Recaptured and Soon

Situation

As Magruder got up to speed on his new command, he found much to concern him. By the time he left Virginia, he had learned that Galveston had been captured and now lay under the guns of a Union fleet. The Union navy in Galveston Harbor was reported to have at least four heavily armed gunboats that had participated in the successful capture of New Orleans. One of these gunboats, USS *Westfield*, was known to have a 100-pounder rifled gun. In addition to the gunboats, the fleet included a mortar schooner that featured a thirteen-inch mortar. These were heavy guns.

Rumors abounded that these naval forces would soon be joined by an infantry force of between fifteen to thirty thousand men to lead the invasion of Texas. The loss of Galveston meant that, as matters now stood, the enemy had a perfect starting place to land troops and supply them by sea. Union possession of Galveston also provided convenient access to a railroad network that extended into the primary settlement area and crop-growing regions of Texas. Magruder knew there were some militia forces and a few thousand

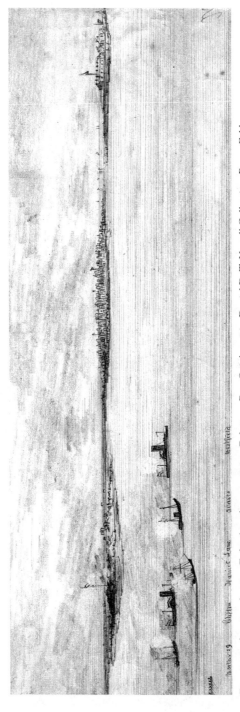

Eyewitness drawing showing Federal gunboats entering Galveston Bay, October 1862. Daniel D. T. Nestell Collection, Box 2, Folder 45. Courtesy of Nimitz Library, United States Naval Academy.

Confederate troops along the Texas coast, as well as a variety of captured artillery pieces, but he did not anticipate having anything like the number of men or guns that he would need to repel a major Union invasion force.

It is more than 1,300 miles from Richmond, Virginia, to Houston, and Magruder's journey, overland because of the Union blockade, was a difficult one. During the long, dusty trip, the general had plenty of time to think and plan. As he studied the map, he became increasingly convinced that he had to find some way to regain control of Galveston. As Magruder later explained to his superiors, "In my judgment, Texas is virtually the Trans-Mississippi Department, and the railroads of Galveston and Houston are virtually Texas. For whoever is the master of the railroads of Galveston and Houston is virtually master of Texas, and this is not the case with any other part of Texas."[14] It was one thing to see the importance of possessing Galveston; it was another to make that possession a reality. The first key question involved timing.

Options

Magruder had three options. He could give up on the idea of recapturing Galveston, or he could wait and see whether an opportunity to retake the city presented itself. Finally, he could force the issue and quickly launch a plan for recapture.

Option 1

Magruder could give up on the idea of reclaiming Galveston. This would essentially be continuing Hébert's policy of falling back and fighting the enemy on the mainland. The Confederacy had never successfully recaptured one of its major port cities once the Union had seized control, and, as the war proceeded, it would not have any greater success in that regard. The Union navy was just too powerful and could bring too many guns to bear against shore fortifications. That was the reason that the Confederacy had, for the most part, concentrated its defensive efforts in the interior. But deciding to abandon Galveston meant giving up the best port in Texas and providing a perfect landing point and supply base for a Union invasion force. If he couldn't find some way to reverse the situation in Galveston, Magruder believed his mission to defend Texas was doomed before it had even begun.

Option 2

Magruder could wait and see whether an opportunity to recapture Galveston presented itself. In many ways, this would be the easiest and most prudent course of action. He was a new commander in a new command. No one would second-guess him if he took some time to get to know his officers and take a thorough inventory of all the available resources. Many commanders would have eased into their new posts and let the situation develop. Maybe the enemy would make a mistake and present Magruder with an opportunity. Maybe the Confederacy would be successful elsewhere and be able to send him the men and armament that General Hébert had repeatedly complained were lacking. Magruder had not been sent to Texas with any instructions to do anything rash or risky. Why take a chance on something until he was forced to do so?

Although Magruder knew he could not be blamed for waiting to see how matters developed, he instinctively knew that passive inaction carried with it substantial risks. He had come from a situation in Virginia where he had been criticized for acting too slowly (Savage's Station) and then too quickly (Malvern Hill). He knew as well as anyone that timing in warfare is everything. On this occasion, timing considerations affected both his forces and the forces available to the enemy.

Magruder quickly learned that one of the most significant forces of experienced Confederates in the Galveston area was a contingent of Sibley's Brigade that was recruiting, drilling, and refitting near Millican in Brazos County. These men were already under orders to be transferred to Louisiana as soon as they were ready for action. Magruder could delay their departure for a short period, but if he did not act quickly, those troops would be unavailable to him. He would have to act fast if he intended to incorporate these soldiers in any battle plan.[15]

The enemy's troops were also an important consideration. Although the Union navy had a commanding position in Galveston Harbor, when Magruder reached Texas, there were no Federal soldiers in the city. Even though Galveston had surrendered, the Confederates maintained effective control of most of the island and basically had unfettered access to the city at night. Magruder knew that the invasion clock was ticking, and that it was only a matter of time before that status changed. Waiting to see how things developed meant giving the enemy the opportunity to land a potentially large force of infantry and cover its advance with fire from the gunboats. Having faced a large Federal army with supporting fire from gunboats at Malvern Hill, Magruder was not eager to repeat that experience. He believed that his plans for recovering Galveston were much more likely to succeed if he acted before the enemy could land additional personnel.

Option 3

Magruder could force the issue and quickly launch a plan to recapture the city. He knew that this course of action, if successful, would go a long way toward redeeming his tarnished reputation. It would also be extremely popular with

Texans, who greeted him as the hero the hour demanded. To show their support for Magruder, the people of Houston had even given him a parade upon his arrival. The parade ended at a stage where thirteen beautiful girls represented the Confederate states, each carrying a sword crowned with a laurel wreath. Such pageantry was difficult for the general to resist. He could see that these were not people who wanted to wait; they expected him to recapture Galveston and actively defend their homes as soon as possible. Governor Lubbock wrote Magruder from Austin, "Can we not do something at Galveston?" This feat would add to Magruder's military reputation, and as Lubbock also observed, "[It will] do much to raise the spirits of our people."[16]

The problem with trying to raise the spirits of the people by recapturing Galveston was that Magruder had arrived in Texas with only a vague plan for accomplishing that task. He did not bring any army with him, nor did he have any Confederate naval fleet to summon. Assembling the resources to initiate any kind of attack against a fleet of Federal gunboats would be challenging. Doing so quickly and launching an assault under the command of men with whom he had never been in battle risked complete disaster. It was a wager that few commanders would have even considered, let alone accepted.

Decision

Magruder decided to force the issue and would waste no time in launching a plan to recapture the city. He arrived in Houston at the end of November fully determined to attack. The only question was how and when. The "when" part of the decision came first. The assault was planned for the evening of December 31, 1862, about a month after Magruder's arrival in Houston. As his principal biographer accurately describes the decision, "none but a Magruder would have attempted such a hazardous undertaking."[17]

Results/Impact

Magruder's sudden attack was crucially important to the way the 1863 Battle of Galveston played out. By striking quickly, Magruder caught his enemy unprepared. As the general expected, the Union was indeed assembling infantry to send to Galveston with the advance portion of an invasion force. The first elements of that force, Companies D, G, and I of the Forty-Second Massachusetts Infantry Regiment, arrived at Galveston on the morning of December 25, 1862. But the three companies amounted to only 249 men and 15 officers. The remainder of the regiment (at least 750 men) was on the way to Galveston, with other regiments eventually intended to follow.[18]

Magruder's decision to act quickly meant that whatever force he could

Officers of the Forty-Second Regiment of Massachusetts Infantry, with Col. Isaac S. Burrell seated at center. Charles P. Bosson, *History of the Forty-Second Regiment* (1886).

come up with would only face a small contingent of enemy infantry. As it turned out, something else important would not be present in Galveston: ammunition. Company G of the Massachusetts troops was armed with Springfield rifles, while Companies D and I had smoothbore muskets. The bulk of the ammunition that had arrived with the three Massachusetts companies on Christmas Day was designed for use in rifles. This mismatch was not a welcome surprise to the regimental officers. In time, other ships carrying ammunition would have arrived, and the ammunition distribution would all have been sorted out. This packing failure was an incredible stroke of good fortune for Magruder. By launching his attack before other troops could arrive, his force outnumbered the Federal infantrymen, only one-third of whom were effectively armed. By acting quickly, Magruder took the infantry largely out of the picture.[19]

Magruder Adopts an Unconventional Battle Plan

Situation

Nothing in Magruder's prior battlefield experience had prepared him to plan and launch an attack on gunboats in a harbor. There was no standard West

Point–approved plan of attack that he could follow. His assault would have to be something unconventional. Magruder knew that he would be going up against a significant number of at least partially armored warships mounting large guns. This meant that he would need to have heavy guns himself and at least some form of naval force to counter the enemy's fleet. These would have to be improvised locally; he was not bringing either of these forces with him from Virginia.

If Magruder was going to attack, he would have to either find or construct his offensive force down in Texas. Magruder had served in south Texas during the Mexican War, but he did not know the area around Galveston very well. He also did not know many of the commanders of his new forces in the area. It would be an enormous challenge to go into a new command in an unfamiliar area and put together the elements of one of the most unusual attacking forces and battle plans of the war. The strategy that Magruder was considering involved simultaneous land and sea attacks on the Federal fleet at night. Even if he could put the pieces together to attempt such a feat, which was highly questionable, the risks were off the chart. The question remained: Was Gen. Magruder confident—or desperate—enough to take such a risk?

Options

Once Magruder decided to recapture Galveston relatively quickly, he had three options. He could launch a more conventional land attack, or he could launch a slightly less conventional one. Alternatively, he could carry out a boldly and wildly unconventional attack.

Option 1

Magruder could launch a more conventional offensive. For example, he could assemble some artillery pieces and move them over to the island. Then, during daylight he could transport them to the waterfront and attack the Federal gunboats. This would eliminate the problems of communication and coordination inherent in simultaneous night attacks by land and sea. A more conventional attack would be much simpler and would not stretch his available resources nearly as far. Magruder also knew a traditional approach would sharply lower the chance of success. A daylight assault coming solely from the shore would not surprise the Federals, and would give their gunboats good visibility to return fire at his land batteries. It did not take a genius to realize that such an attack stood little chance of success. In some ways, a direct strike during daylight would be repeating the general's mistake at Malvern Hill.

Option 2

Magruder could carry out a slightly less conventional attack that was not quite as far a stretch. For example, he could attempt a simultaneous assault by land and sea during daylight hours. This would significantly increase his chances of successfully coordinating the action, and it would also give his gunners easily visible enemy vessels to target. Once again, however, an attack during the day would involve less of an element of surprise. Also, moving guns into position along the waterfront would almost certainly be difficult under active enemy fire. If Magruder's gunners could see the enemy ships better, the Federal gunners on those ships could see his own artillery batteries better. This option seemed to have all of the risks of a bolder attack with even less chance of success.

Option 3

Magruder could resort to an unconventional operation that involved simultaneous night attacks by land and sea. This risky option would be extremely difficult to implement. Night attacks were relatively rare during the Civil War, and simultaneous assaults involving gunboats and land forces were almost unheard of. Offensives involving improvised cottonclad gunboats as part of such a large-scale coordinated strike did not occur at any other time or place during the war. The enemy would not expect such an attack, but it was not at all clear that Magruder could pull something like this together, particularly on short notice.

Decision

Although it was risky and challenging, Magruder believed that the plan of attack with the most unconventional elements probably stood the greatest chance of success. The enemy would be surprised and would hopefully not be positioned to respond. In putting together the basic strategies for this assault, Magruder had some important assistance from local experts. During the long journey from Richmond to Texas, he traveled with Maj. Caleb G. Forshey, an engineer who had taught at a military school for boys in Galveston before the war. Forshey suggested transferring artillery pieces to the waterfront one night and launching a surprise attack on the gunboats from the shore. Then, while the gunboats were focused on the shore batteries, some improvised Confederate gunboats would approach the Federal fleet from the rear and force it to evacuate the harbor. When members of Magruder's staff questioned whether this bold plan was feasible, Forshey responded, "General, I think the best plan is to resolve to retake it, and then canvass the difficulties."

Forshey later followed this conversation with a more detailed memo spelling out his proposed strategy.[20]

While Magruder was pondering Forshey's proposal, it received support from an unexpected source. As he crossed the Sabine River on his way to Houston, the general encountered Capt. Armand R. Wier of Company B, Cook's First Texas Heavy Artillery. Wier volunteered to place his guns on steamboats operating in the commercial traffic on the river, and to attempt to clear the Union blockaders from the entrance to Sabine Pass. In his official report, Magruder would later credit Wier and his men as the "first volunteers for the desperate enterprise of expelling the enemy's fleets from our waters."[21]

The characterization of this plan as a "desperate enterprise" is entirely accurate. Magruder decided to launch an attack incorporating the bold and risky elements suggested by Forshey and Wier and involving concurrent assaults by land and sea at night. In fact, Magruder would later add even more unconventional elements, such as a wading charge against Union troops on a wharf and a railroad-mounted artillery piece. Hoping to increase the element of surprise and catch his enemy off guard, the general scheduled the offensive for New Year's Eve of 1862–63.

Results/Impact

Magruder's decision to implement the unconventional battle plan in its entirety led directly to Confederate success in the Battle of Galveston. The strategy's many alternative means of attack meant that some could fail without ending the Confederates' chances. This was important. As it turned out, many of the key pieces of the plan did fail, but Magruder still ended up with a victory.

The Confederate attack was originally to begin at midnight, with the fire of the land batteries signaling the naval attack on the rear of the gunboats to commence. However, Magruder was late getting his artillery pieces over to the waterfront, and he did not achieve his goal of simultaneously attacking the enemy from the land and shore. If he had just relied on a bombardment from the shore, that action would have been unsuccessful—indeed, was unsuccessful—at driving the enemy's warships from the harbor.

If Magruder had attempted to implement his battle plan during daylight it would also have failed. One of the principal reasons the Union warships performed so poorly during the battle was that they had difficulty maneuvering through unfamiliar waters at night. In fact, as discussed below, the Union flagship and its commander ran aground and were out of action for the entire battle. It turned out that the audacity of Magruder's unconventional plan was critical to the successful outcome of the battle. The scheme that some of his staff officers initially dismissed as crazy proved to be one of the most remarkably successful attacks of the war.

Magruder Puts Leon Smith in Charge of His Naval Force

Situation

Although Magruder arrived in Houston intending to assault the Federal gunboats from the rear with his own gunboats, he did not have any gunboats. In fact, there were very few officers of the Confederate navy in the area. If he wanted to use a naval force, he would have to create one.

Magruder was not entirely unfamiliar with ships and nautical warfare. While on the Virginia Peninsula, he had been very close to the site of the famous battle between the ironclads *Monitor* and *Virginia*. He did not have the time or the iron to create similar ironclad vessels in Texas. What Magruder did have were a number of packet steamboats and storehouses full of cotton bales. He decided to use both to create a small fleet of "cottonclad" steamers to serve as Confederate gunboats. Cotton bales were stacked high on the decks to serve as protective barricades. These vessels, armored with Capt. Armand Wier's artillery pieces in their bows, would be the force to attack the Union gunboats from the rear. Magruder knew that this fleet could be the difference in winning or losing the engagement. This left the important questions of who should be placed in charge of building it and then leading it in battle?

Options

Magruder could appoint one of several figures to command the cottonclad warships: the chief Confederate naval officer in the area, a member of his own staff or an army officer, or someone outside the Confederate army and navy.

Option 1

Magruder could designate the foremost Confederate naval officer in the vicinity to equip and command the cottonclad flotilla. That officer was Cmdr. William W. Hunter. Although born in Pennsylvania, Hunter had joined the Confederate navy from Louisiana after resigning from the US Navy. He had experience in the naval arena, and he would seem to be the logical choice except for one problem. Hunter had already exhibited difficulty dealing with Confederate army officers in the area.[22]

Magruder did not know Hunter well, and placing an unknown and unliked officer in charge of an improvised naval operation was risky. However, there was an even bigger problem. It turned out that Hunter was a particularly bad fit for the operation, because he had already gone on record as declaring that he did not consider the *Bayou City* suited for a gunboat.[23] *Bayou City* was one of the two boats that Magruder intended to use as the centerpiece of his naval operation. Allowing a man he did not know to command a force that he had already declared a failure seemed to be a bad idea.

Option 2

Magruder could appoint one of his staff or an army officer to command the boats. The advantage of this option was that the general would know and presumably trust the person he placed in command. The disadvantage was that the individual in charge of the naval action would not have any real maritime experience. The risk of choosing an inexperienced person to lead a night naval action against the Federal fleet was obvious. If this decision failed, Magruder knew that he would be severely criticized. What he really needed was somebody with maritime experience whom he knew and trusted.

Option 3

Magruder could find a commander outside the army and navy. That person would need to be someone with maritime experience and someone reliable. If this person was not already in the Confederate army or navy, perhaps such an appointment would avoid being hampered by the bureaucracy of each service. But if he chose someone with no prior military experience and the operation went badly, Magruder knew that he would elicit sharp criticism. There was no way around it. The general would face a difficult dilemma in deciding who should lead the naval part of his plan.

Decision

General Magruder decided to place Capt. Leon Smith in charge of his naval operations for recapturing Galveston. Magruder had long been acquainted with Smith, a merchant ship captain whom he had encountered while stationed in California. The general knew Smith to have great experience in steamboat management. Magruder quickly employed him as a "major" in the quartermaster's department, making him a volunteer aide on his staff.[24]

Placing Leon Smith in charge of the major naval offensive operation of this campaign was one of the best decisions Magruder ever made. Smith had been unofficially serving with the Confederate army since early in the war, and he had been in command of the *General Rusk*, which regularly patrolled the waters of Galveston Bay. His appointment was a popular choice. One

Maj. Leon Smith, CSA. Name File—
Photograph Collection. Rosenberg
Library, Galveston, Texas.

early history of Galveston praised Smith's "great daring and well-known skill as a navigator," and both of these qualities would be tested in the Battle of Galveston.[25]

Results/Impact

Smith's appointment was key to the outcome of the Battle of Galveston. The engagement would not have been won without Smith's Confederate naval force and its persistent attacks on the Union fleet. Leon Smith turned out to be the ideal person to command the Confederate fleet.

After his selection to command, Commodore Smith, as he soon became known, wasted no time in working night and day to get the cottonclad gunboats ready for action. Magruder admitted in his official report after the battle, "Too much credit cannot be bestowed on Commodore Leon Smith, whose professional ability, energy, and perseverance amidst many discouraging influences were so conspicuously displayed in the preparation for the attack, while in its execution his heroism was sublime."[26] Magruder's decision to put an outsider in command of the key element of his plan turned out to be an inspired one.

Farragut Decides Not to Allow Renshaw to Withdraw His Union Naval Force

Situation

Magruder's strategy to attack the Union position at Galveston was not the complete surprise he had wished for. In fact, various reports about the forces that Magruder was assembling soon reached the ears of Cmdr. William B. Renshaw, who served as commodore of the Union fleet at Galveston. Renshaw forwarded these rumors and accounts to his superior, Adm. David G. Farragut, along with requests to either strongly reinforce him or allow him to withdraw from Galveston Harbor and resume blockading off the entrance to Galveston Bay. Renshaw was particularly concerned about reports that Magruder had obtained some heavy artillery pieces that might be fired at his fleet in Galveston's shallow harbor from relatively close range. Renshaw warned Farragut, "I can see no reason why we can't be made to withdraw, for beyond a doubt they have two 84-pounders (I at first thought them 64-pounder rifles) of greater range than any guns we have."[27]

Options

Faced with Renshaw's dire warnings about enemy plans, Farragut had two choices: he could grant Renshaw's request to withdraw from the harbor and

Cmdr. William Bainbridge Renshaw, USN. NH 66699. US Naval History and Heritage Command.

resume the blockade outside the entrance to Galveston Bay, or he could instruct Renshaw to stay where he was and defend his position as best he could.

Option 1

Farragut could authorize Renshaw to withdraw. If Renshaw was right about the enemy's plans, moving the gunboats would place them in a more protected and defensible position. Then, when Union reinforcements finally arrived in Texas, the city could be retaken. This was the safest option, but it meant giving back the largest city and best port in Texas without a fight before recapturing it again once the enemy had fortified it more securely. The army had been promising Farragut that infantry forces were on their way to Galveston, and it might well be that the new troops would arrive soon and render Renshaw's concerns moot. For these reasons, Farragut was reluctant to go along with any proposal to change course and withdraw the fleet from Galveston Harbor.

Option 2

Farragut could instruct Renshaw to stay where he was and defend his position as best he could. The admiral was not sure what to make of Renshaw's frantic reports about enemy plans to attack his gunboats, thinking they might be exaggerated bits of fancy. But he was certain that he would face severe criticism from his superiors and the press if he agreed to a withdrawal without being forced to do so. Farragut told Renshaw as much in an angry letter:

> Has it come to this, that four gunboats armed with 8, 9, and 11-inch guns are to be driven out of a harbor by the report of some "reliable person" that preparations are making to drive them out of the harbor? Are you willing, captain, that I should make such a statement to the honorable Secretary—that we have abandoned the ports of Texas because of reports that they were making preparations to drive us out? I trust not."[28]

In deciding whether to grant Renshaw' request to withdraw his gunboats, Admiral Farragut was probably thinking about more than the situation at Galveston. He only had to pick up a newspaper to be reminded that December 1862 was one of the lowest points of the war for the Lincoln administration and the Union military effort. The midterm elections had resulted in heavy losses for the Republicans. To compound the political disasters, the Union military had not done much to distinguish itself recently. After being forced away from the gates of Richmond in the summer of 1862, Union armies in the East seemed to have severe difficulties achieving any material success on the battlefield. The Battle of Fredericksburg, fought in the middle of December, was a stunning defeat that led Lincoln to replace his commanding general once again. A week later, a caucus of frustrated cabinet members initiated a crisis in an attempt to force out Secretary of State William Seward and take control of the war effort. Although Lincoln's Emancipation Proclamation was scheduled to take effect on January 1, 1863, there was rampant speculation that the defeats at Fredericksburg and the crisis in the government might even force the postponement or revocation of that controversial action.

As bad as things were in the East, the situation in the West was not much better. Union armies were barely moving in Tennessee, and there seemed to be no serious threat to Braxton Bragg's Army of Mississippi. The Confederates still had firm control of Vicksburg on the Mississippi River, and Grant's efforts to launch a series of indirect operations to force Vicksburg to surrender had so far proved unsuccessful. To make matters even worse, on December 20, 1862, Gen. Earl Van Dorn, formerly in charge of the Confederate defenses of Texas, led a strikingly effective cavalry raid on Grant's most important Union supply depot at Holly Springs, Mississippi. This caused Grant to withdraw to Memphis and postponed plans to capture Vicksburg until 1863 at the earliest.

All in all, one of the few sources of consistently good news coming to Washington was Farragut's naval operations on the Gulf Coast. As the admiral had proudly boasted, the key cities on the Texas coast finally seemed to be under Union control and were just awaiting Federal occupation troops. Texas seemed to be on the verge of becoming a fully conquered Rebel territory. It was one of the few real success stories. It is thus understandable that Farragut was extremely reluctant to do anything that would detract from this happy picture. Even it if might be justified from a purely military standpoint, allowing Galveston, the most important Confederate city in Texas, to fall back into Rebel hands without a fight simply was not something that the admiral could accept.

Decision

Farragut ordered Renshaw to stay where he was and defend his position: "The gunboats must hold Galveston until the army arrives, and I have no doubt when you are attacked you will make a defense that will do credit to the Navy as well as to yourselves." It is interesting to note that Farragut said "*when* you are attacked" rather than "*if* you are attacked." This suggests that the admiral knew perfectly well that Renshaw's force was about to find itself in danger.[29]

Adm. David G. Farragut, USN.
LC-DIG-ppmsca-40658. Library
of Congress.

Results/Impact

Renshaw's concerns were soon determined to be well founded. As it turned out, when the Confederates attacked, the Union fleet found itself at relatively short distance from Confederate guns in a shallow harbor that did not allow for easy maneuvering. Magruder's battle plan depended on taking advantage of the fleet's vulnerable position in the harbor and striking it from the front and the rear. That plan would not have been possible if the Union fleet had been stationed—as Renshaw strongly urged—at the entrance to the bay. At the position Renshaw preferred, Confederate artillery would have been less of a threat, and enemy gunboats could not easily have attacked from behind.

Although Farragut probably never admitted it to anybody but himself, his refusal of Renshaw's withdrawal request led directly to the humiliating defeat at the Battle of Galveston. That battle, which Farragut himself characterized as one of the most shameful disasters in the navy's history, also led to the loss of two gunboats, along with Renshaw and some very promising officers. Farragut's decision to keep the fleet in Galveston Harbor led to a battle that resulted in Confederate occupation of the city for the remainder of the war.

Alternate Decision/Scenario

It is difficult to forecast what might have happened if Farragut had granted Renshaw's request. One possibility is that Magruder would have used the delay from any withdrawal, as he ultimately did, to fortify the city enough that it would not have been easily captured. If events had played out this way, Farragut's decision to allow Renshaw to withdraw would have saved the casualties experienced during the Battle of Galveston, but it would not have had much wider significance.

But some of the potential alternatives involved consequences that extended beyond Texas. Another plausible scenario is that the reinforced Union troops would have reentered Galveston Bay at a later time and used the city as they had originally intended, making it a launching point for a Union invasion of Texas. If things had turned out that way, a successful Union incursion into Texas might have taken place in 1863. As discussed in greater detail later, a successful invasion of the state that year might have paved the way to an earlier attack on Mobile, Alabama (one of the alternates to a Texas campaign that was actively considered in late 1863). Striking Mobile sooner might have had important ramifications for the later conduct of the war.[30]

Renshaw Decides Not to Destroy the Railroad Bridge

Situation

When Commodore Renshaw first entered Galveston Bay and took possession of the city, he noted the railroad bridge stretching between Eagle Grove on the island and Virginia Point on the mainland. He estimated that the Confederate fort on the mainland (Fort Hébert) was garrisoned by three to five thousand men. There was also a Confederate fort near Eagle Grove, but Renshaw did not hazard a guess as to the number of its defenders. He believed that although it would be difficult, some of his vessels could be lightened enough to get within range of the fort and possibly destroy the bridge.[31]

As the Union occupation continued, it became obvious to both sides that the railroad bridge to the mainland was a very strategic resource. If planked over, it could potentially be used to transport Confederate artillery pieces from the mainland to attack the city and the Union gunboats in its harbor. Likewise, the bridge could be used to transport Union soldiers and their supplies over from the island to the mainland as part of the planned invasion force leading toward Houston and the Texas heartland. Both Federals and Confederates had reasons to see the bridge kept intact, and both saw scenarios under which it could prove very valuable to their enemy. It seemed only a matter of time before one side or the other would determine that the bridge must be destroyed.

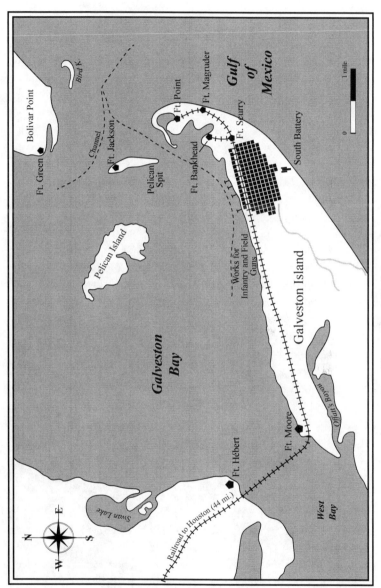

Fortifications at Galveston (1863)

Options

Renshaw had two options: he could attempt to demolish the railroad bridge, or he could hold off on attacking it and see how matters developed.

Option 1

Renshaw could launch an attack on the bridge and attempt to destroy it. He had initially determined not to prioritize taking down the bridge, apparently calculating that its benefits as an invasion route outweighed its threat. He also hoped that the arrival of more soldiers might mean that the army could march out of the city in force and take control of Eagle Grove and the bridge.

As time went on, however, and Renshaw became increasingly concerned about enemy plans to attack him, he began seriously considering options to destroy the bridge. This would have been more difficult than it might sound today. The soldiers from the Forty-Second Massachusetts regiment who later arrived were eventually enlisted in an effort to settle on some joint plan to attack the fort at Eagle Grove. But they reported that "none of the Union naval vessels could get near enough to do any permanent damage, on account of the narrow, tortuous and shallow channel." The gunboats at Galveston apparently did not have any armed launches, only small rowboats that could not have mounted any substantial artillery pieces. Although the Massachusetts troops began assembling the materials that would be necessary to blow up and burn the bridge, they waited on further reinforcements to attempt the hazardous march down the island to attack the Confederates at Eagle Grove. By December 29, the Confederates had reinforced the garrison at Eagle Grove, making such an attack even riskier.[32]

Option 2

Renshaw could hold off on any attack against the bridge, hoping that it would prove unnecessary or that reinforcements would enable the army to act soon and without endangering any of his vessels. Any plan to capture or destroy the bridge with his current forces might not succeed, and it might risk men and guns that he could not spare if the enemy attacked as he feared. Doing nothing in this case was probably the safest choice for a naval commander with limited exposure to land operations. If this gamble paid off, the bridge might wind up as a useful invasion route. If Renshaw was wrong, however, and the enemy could make effective use of the bridge, it could potentially lead to disaster.

Decision

Renshaw held off on taking any direct action to attack or destroy the bridge. Not all of his officers were happy with this decision. Capt. J. M. Wainwright of the USS *Harriet Lane* was strongly in favor of doing something to ruin the bridge. He and Col. Isaac Burrell of the Massachusetts regiment had outlined a plan to put some small guns in boats and get them within range where they could potentially shell the fort at Eagle Grove while the Massachusetts troops attacked by land. But the scheme was risky, and Renshaw would not approve the operation until all the details had been carefully worked out. Although time ran out on this plan, the Massachusetts regimental history later reported that "an attempt [to destroy the bridge] would have been made had not the event of January 1st [the Battle of Galveston] occurred."[33]

Results/Impact

Renshaw's decision not to at least attempt to destroy the railroad bridge proved catastrophic. It is likely that when Galveston was first captured, and General Hébert removed most of his forces to the mainland, the bridge could have been severed. Captain Wainwright and the Massachusetts troops certainly believed that a small joint operation conducted even later in December could have accomplished the same intended result.

If the success probability of destroying the bridge was somewhat uncertain, the consequences of its remaining intact for use by the Confederates were very clear. At dusk on December 31, 1862, Magruder's soldiers moved approximately twenty-one large guns across the planked-over railroad bridge and began a circuitous march to the waterfront, where the artillery pieces were distributed at strategic positions extending along the bayfront for about two and a half miles. One of the guns was a large naval gun mounted on a railroad car. The Battle of Galveston would be only the second Civil War battle in which rail-mounted artillery was used. Magruder had first employed rail-mounted artillery, which the Confederates called the "Land *Merrimack*," at the Battle of Savage's Station (June 29, 1862).[34]

Without the intact bridge, the Battle of Galveston would not have been fought on Galveston Island. Magruder would have been unable to move his guns to the waterfront in time to launch an attack coordinated with his gunboats. Moving so many large guns over to the island by boat would have been impractical. As it turned out, even with the aid of the railroad bridge, Magruder was late getting the guns to their assigned positions. But shortly after 4:00 a.m. on New Year's Day, Magruder fired the first cannon, signaling the beginning of the Battle of Galveston. Magruder's bombardment, the most important land-attack of his battle plan, would not have been possible without the continued existence of the railroad bridge.[35] Without the intact bridge, the Battle of Galveston simply would not have occurred as and when it did.

Renshaw Investigates a Light in the Distance

Situation

At approximately 1:30 a.m. on January 1, lookouts on board the *Westfield* and *Clifton* saw lights in the distance up the channels to the north. These lights were likely from the cottonclad steamboats under the command of Leon Smith. In accordance with his instructions, Smith delayed in launching any attack because Magruder had not yet arrived with the artillery and signaled the beginning of the operation. Having been warned of a potential Confederate offensive, Renshaw was naturally interested in what this strange traffic in the distance might be. There was only one way to learn what the lights represented; one of his vessels needed to venture into the dark waters and investigate.

Options

Renshaw had two options. He could order one of the other gunboats to go investigate, or he could take *Westfield*, his own flagship, and go determine the source of the strange lights himself.

Option 1

Renshaw could send one of his other gunboats to investigate. This errand would probably fall to *Clifton*, another shallow-draft ferryboat that had been converted into a lightly armored gunboat. *Clifton* was nearby and had already spotted the same lights in the distance. The advantage of sending this boat was that Renshaw could stay in position with the rest of the fleet and be available if any important orders needed to be issued. The disadvantage of sending *Clifton* was that he might be ordering it to face an unknown number of enemy warships. If there were decisions that needed to be made about how or even whether to engage the Confederates, Renshaw strongly preferred to be the one who was on the scene to make them.

Option 2

Renshaw could take *Westfield* and investigate the strange lights in person. The advantage of doing this was that by going himself, he would presumably have the most accurate and current information about the enemy ships and their plans. The disadvantage of this decision was that if something went wrong and *Westfield* was removed from action when the enemy attacked, the Federal fleet would suddenly be deprived of its commander and one of its most powerful warships.

USS *Westfield*. Drawing by R. G. Skerrett, 1904. NH 48488. US Naval History and Heritage Command.

Decision

Renshaw decided to take *Westfield* and track down the strange lights himself. The result was catastrophic. After spending months in Galveston Bay, Renshaw was well aware that it featured many sections where the channels were very narrow, and even the edges of the channels were very shallow. It was not a good idea to be going through unfamiliar portions of these waters at night, especially since *Westfield* had such a bad habit of running aground. Sailors in the fleet joked that Renshaw kept *Clifton* around primarily to act as a tug to pull *Westfield* off when it ran aground on obstacles.[36]

Results/Impact

Few decisions played a greater part in the disastrous outcome of this battle than Renshaw's ill-advised choice to go see the source of the strange lights himself. Shortly after Renshaw left to investigate the lights, *Westfield* ran aground near Pelican Spit and signaled *Clifton* to come pull it out of danger. While *Clifton* was repeatedly unsuccessful in helping *Westfield* get free and afloat, the Confederate bombardment started in the distance. The Battle of Galveston had begun, and Renshaw would play no part in its action.

The commander was helpless. At the worst possible time, and on the worst possible night, Renshaw found himself and his flagship stranded away from the rest of the fleet and unable to monitor developments and communicate with subordinates. Because *Westfield* was out of action, the Federal fleet was without direction during the most critical parts of the battle. It was also without the services of one of its most powerful and experienced gunboats. At the conclusion of the fighting, Renshaw would be forced to blow up *Westfield* to keep it out of Confederate hands, in the process killing himself and more than a dozen members of his crew.

Magruder Launches a Wading Charge against Kuhn's Wharf

Situation

Magruder knew that the soldiers of the Forty-Second Massachusetts had been positioned at the end of Kuhn's Wharf. That historic structure was at the foot of Eighteenth Street, placing it fairly near what would ultimately be the center of the Confederate line of battle. Kuhn's Wharf, one of the first built in Galveston, was approximately four hundred feet long. It terminated in a triangular dock adjacent to a two-story warehouse. Under the direction of Col. Isaac Burrell, the Massachusetts soldiers had removed planks from

Photograph of Kuhn's Wharf taken from the top of the Hendley Building at Twentieth and Strand, 1861. Rosenberg Library, Galveston, Texas.

the wharf near shore and created a series of barricades to prevent an enemy force from charging down and assaulting their position. Burrell had been promised that if the Confederates attacked in force, the navy would send boats in five minutes' time and transport the infantry to a more secure location. This promise would never be kept.[37]

From scouting expeditions in the city, Magruder knew about the fortified Union position on Kuhn's Wharf and the missing planks that prevented a direct assault down the wharf. It is unlikely, however, that Magruder knew about the Massachusetts regiment's lack of ammunition. What he did know was that his artillery batteries during the battle would be situated on a long string of isolated positions, sometimes street corners, along the waterfront. Magruder's plan called for the guns to be moved there during the night, so there would be no time to fortify those sites. He was understandably concerned that during the battle the Massachusetts troops might suddenly attempt to come ashore and threaten one or more of his artillery positions on the waterfront. To free Galveston from Union control, Magruder believed that he needed to find some way to capture or otherwise neutralize the infantry force on Kuhn's Wharf. But what was the best way to accomplish this objective?

Options

Magruder had two options. He could leave the Massachusetts troops alone and not plan to attack them. The other alternative was to devise some unconventional attack that might neutralize them or secure their surrender.

Option 1

Magruder could leave the Massachusetts troops alone and hope that they would not be a factor in the battle. On the surface, this had some appeal. After all, the main threat in Galveston Harbor was the Union gunboats. The small force of Union infantry was heavily outnumbered and (although Magruder probably didn't know it) extremely short of ammunition. Ignoring these Federals posed two problems. As mentioned previously, the infantry might throw a wrench in the Confederate plan by storming ashore at an inconvenient moment and capturing one or more of the artillery batteries firing out at the Federal fleet. The other problem with ignoring the Massachusetts soldiers would emerge if the Confederates ended up losing the battle or not fully securing the bay so that some Federal warships remained. The Union infantry would then be in a favorable position to lead the effort to recapture the city once reinforcements arrived.

Option 2

Magruder could devise some unconventional plan of attack that might secure the capture or surrender of the Federals. The problem with any such solution here was that it necessarily involved an attack at night in the midst of a bombardment in which both sides were firing at relatively short range. Magruder considered launching a wading charge on both sides of the wharf. But these men would be entirely unprotected as they advanced. The exposed troops would have guns firing behind them, in front of them, and conceivably from straight above them. Some of Magruder's men would be wading while carrying lengthy ladders. Thus this plan involved a high degree of risk.

Decision

Believing that he had a real opportunity to capture the Union troops under the cover of battle, Magruder launched an unconventional attack against Kuhn's Wharf. Magruder first sent a force of sharpshooters and a small artillery piece down an adjacent wharf and attempted to fire at the end of Kuhn's Wharf from the side. This action was of limited effectiveness and was intended primarily to serve as a diversion.

The real attack materialized when Col. Joseph Cook led five hundred Confederates in a wading charge on both sides of the wharf. The soldiers were carrying scaling ladders, and the plan was to wade out to the end of the wharf, mount the wharf from both sides, and attack the Union troops from the rear. The inspiration for this plan was probably the Mexican War, in which Magruder had played a significant part. That war had seen American troops successfully use ladders to assault supposedly impregnable positions near Mexico City. Yet ladders did not work as well at Galveston as they had in the Mexican War. Cook's wading charge at Galveston was probably the largest such assault of the Civil War. It was also a complete failure because the ladders sank down in the mud and were too short to reach the top of the wharf. [38]

Results/Impact

Although Magruder's unorthodox attack at Kuhn's Wharf did not directly capture Burrell's position, it kept the Massachusetts commander from considering any counterattack against the Confederate gun positions on the shore. It kept Magruder's batteries from being assaulted by land and allowed them to continue firing at the Federal fleet from their exposed positions. Although the wading charge was unsuccessful in reaching the top of the wharf, it effectively isolated the Union troops and inhibited potential efforts to rescue them by boat. Deprived of any real options, the Massachusetts soldiers stayed down behind their barricade and suffered remarkably few casualties during the battle. The Confederates suffered quite a few casualties during the disastrous offensive. Despite the failure of the wading charge, Magruder would accomplish his objective. With no way off the wharf, Colonel Burrell eventually surrendered his force near the end of the Battle of Galveston.[39]

Leon Smith Continues His Naval Attack

Situation

As daylight approached on January 1, 1863, things were going badly for Magruder. The Confederate batteries were being silenced or driven back to shelter behind brick buildings in the city. The wading charge against Kuhn's Wharf had ended in failure. The land portion of the Confederate attack was on the edge of defeat, and the naval part of the attack had never even begun. Over at Magruder's headquarters, there was nothing but depression and disappointment.[40]

Although Magruder did not know it, there was still hope for the naval part of his plan. As earlier witnessed in the distance by Commodore Renshaw, Leon Smith and his cottonclads had indeed arrived within sight of the Federal fleet at midnight. This was the appointed hour for the coordinated attack. The Confederate steamers had only retreated when Magruder's bombardment from the land was delayed. When Magruder finally pulled the lanyard to fire the gun that started the action, Smith and his cottonclads resumed their slow movement against the rear of the Federal fleet. As with the land portion of the Confederate battle plans, things went wrong almost immediately.[41]

The Confederate fleet consisted of two steamers (*Neptune No. 2* and *Bayou City*) that had been converted into cottonclad gunboats. Capt. Armand Wier, the first volunteer for the expedition, was in the bow of *Bayou City* with a 32-pounder rifled gun. As he fired his fourth shot, the gun exploded, killing him and taking out of action the only serious piece of artillery on either of the cottonclads. This meant that Smith's only remaining method of attack was to get close enough to the Union gunboats for his sharpshooters to sweep the decks with small-arms fire. If he could actually ram one of the enemy vessels, he might then send over a boarding party. As he confessed to one of the sharpshooters, "Our only chance is to get alongside before they hit us."[42]

Ramming a Union gunboat had always been a risky but necessary option in Smith's plan of attack. Indeed, that was the principal reason that he had so many sharpshooters aboard. On the hurricane deck (an upper deck) of each cottonclad he had erected two landing stages, or boarding planks, leaning

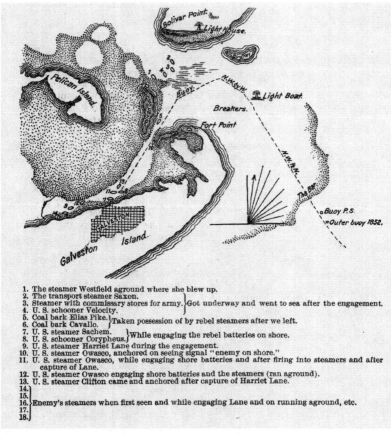

1. The steamer Westfield aground where she blew up.
2. The transport steamer Saxon.
3. Steamer with commissary stores for army. }Got underway and went to sea after the engagement.
4. U. S. schooner Velocity.
5. Coal bark Elias Pike. }Taken possession of by rebel steamers after we left.
6. Coal bark Cavallo. }
7. U. S. steamer Sachem. }While engaging the rebel batteries on shore.
8. U. S. schooner Corypheus. }
9. U. S. steamer Harriet Lane during the engagement.
10. U. S. steamer Owasco, anchored on seeing signal "enemy on shore."
11. U. S. steamer Owasco, while engaging shore batteries and after firing into steamers and after capture of Lane.
12. U. S. steamer Owasco engaging shore batteries and the steamers (ran aground).
13. U. S. steamer Clifton came and anchored after capture of Harriet Lane.
14. }
15. }
16. }Enemy's steamers when first seen and while engaging Lane and on running aground, etc.
17. }
18. }

Diagram of attack on Federal fleet at Galveston, January 1, 1863, from *Official Records of the Union and Confederate Navies*, volume 19.

outward with anchors or grapnels on their ends. The idea was that when the vessels got close enough, the rope suspending the stage would be cut, and the stage would then crash down on the enemy vessel, providing a useful ramp for the sharpshooters to rush aboard and capture their opponent. Historian Andrew Hall has observed that this device mimicked the Roman *corvus* from classical times.[43]

The first Union ship that Smith encountered turned out to be the former revenue cutter *Harriet Lane*, probably the most formidable warship in Galveston Harbor. The *Lane* was a side-wheel steamer, which meant that it had a paddle wheel situated on each of its sides. These wheels were convenient targets for vessels like the cottonclads that would be attempting to ram them.

The ebbing tide was strong, and it was difficult for Leon Smith to maneuver his heavy cottonclads so that they could confront the enemy ship as planned. Finally, however, they were in position to launch their attack. The strategy was for the cottonclads to assault a side-wheel steamer like the *Harriet Lane* by ramming their bows into the area around the wheels on each side, hopefully disabling the vessel. Then the boarding parties would storm onto the enemy ship and seize control. This plan went wrong almost from the first minute.

Bayou City, Smith's flagship, was the first to attempt ramming the *Lane*. Smith missed his objective, and *Bayou City* swept under the *Lane*'s port bow. As soon as the cottonclad got close, the sharpshooters cut the rope holding the landing stage as they had been instructed, and it plunged down. Missing the Union ship entirely, the structure instead struck the water and was dragged back, in the process disabling the Confederate boat's wheelhouse. The first ramming attempt had been a complete disaster.[44]

On the opposite side, *Neptune* prepared for its own attempt to ram and board the *Lane*. Unlike *Bayou City*, *Neptune* managed to solidly hit the Union vessel. Unfortunately for the Confederates, the ramming effort did little injury to their opponent. Instead, the collision damaged the ramming ship so severely that its captain was forced to withdraw from the action. He deliberately ran *Neptune* aground near Thirty-Second Street, where the ship sank. The second ramming attempt had been an even bigger disaster for the Confederates than the first.[45]

Time was running out for Leon Smith and his rapidly dwindling force. Over on *Bayou City*, the wheelhouse had been finally cleared to the extent that the cottonclad could again be steered. Leon Smith could launch yet another attack if he dared. But should he?

Options

Leon Smith had two options: he could continue to press his attack on *Harriet Lane* and the remainder of the Federal fleet, or he could withdraw from combat and save his remaining ship and men.

Option 1

Smith could use *Bayou City* to try ramming *Harriet Lane* yet again. If this third attempt succeeded, the loss of *Neptune* meant that he would now have only his own boat to deal with the remainder of the Federal fleet. But there was still the chance that Smith might board the *Lane* and seize control, which would then give him two ships to continue the action. Indeed, if he captured the *Lane*, perhaps he would so scare the Union fleet officers that they might leave the harbor. Smith knew that such a course of action was risky, but he also knew that the battle was lost if he did not at least attempt to continue his attack.

Option 2

Smith could discontinue the action and steam away, keeping his vessel and men safe for another battle in the future. To most commanders, this would have been an appealing option. Smith could not have been encouraged by his status. Half his force of gunboats was now sunk. Not only had both prior ramming attempts proved unsuccessful, one of his landing stages was disabled, and he now had no effective artillery to keep the enemy at a distance. Even if Smith managed to board or disable the *Lane*, it was highly uncertain how his reduced force could possibly prevail against the remaining Union gunboats.

As Smith pondered his options, the one thing he knew with certainty was that Magruder and the artillery force ashore still counted on him continuing to press the attack. The whole Confederate plan to force the Federal fleet out of the harbor relied on the combination of a shore bombardment from one side and a naval attack from the other. If one part of this combined assault ceased, the whole enterprise would fail. Smith also knew that if he withdrew, he would be leaving the crew of the sunken *Neptune* to an uncertain fate that might include capture or death.

Decision

Leon "the Lion" Smith, as he subsequently became known to Texans, was nothing if not bold. He decided to use *Bayou City* to launch a third ramming attempt against *Harriet Lane*. He knew that during the prior efforts, the Confederate sharpshooters and their shotguns must have killed or disabled a number of the *Lane*'s crewmen with their small-arms fire. The *Lane* had not yet fired a broadside at him, leading Smith to believe that another ramming attempt from the side might still be successful. He ordered the movement and waited anxiously for its result.

As *Harriet Lane* backed its engines, *Bayou City* finally struck the Union vessel solidly near its port paddle wheel. The collision caused the frame of the *Lane*'s port wheel to rebound and punch into the deck of *Bayou City*. In addition, the *Lane*'s cathead was shot away, and its anchor inadvertently deployed.

"Surprise and Capture of the United States Steamer *Harriet Lane* by the Confederates under General Magruder." Line engraving from *The Soldier in Our Civil War*, volume 2 (1885). NH 59142. US Naval History and Heritage Command.

Unable to use his remaining boarding stage because of its position, Smith and his men then swarmed over the *Lane*'s boarding nets, and within seconds the *Lane*'s remaining officers and crew were either killed or captured.[46]

Smith and the Confederate cottonclads had succeeded in their objective of capturing *Harriet Lane*, but the ramming attempt had placed them in a difficult spot. The collision had left *Harriet Lane* and *Bayou City* locked in an almost perpendicular position and anchored. Smith's fleet now included three warships (*Bayou City*, *Neptune No. 2*, and *Harriet Lane*), but none of them were currently capable of movement. What made matters worse was that in the darkness, Confederate gunners onshore were continuing to fire at the *Lane*, while some of the Union gunboats were now also firing at the interlocked vessels. Smith was effectively under fire from both sides. To buy some time, he ordered his troops to sound the Rebel yell to alert Confederates on the shore of his position. He also ordered the enemy prisoners to be prominently displayed on deck to deter firing from the Union fleet.[47]

Smith's actions had temporarily kept both sides from firing on his immobile vessels. But how would the battle proceed from this point? Smith knew that his best chance of success was to keep pressure on the Federals.

He sent Capt. Henry S. Lubbock and the *Lane*'s senior surviving officer over to the Federal fleet in a small boat under a flag of truce and demanded their surrender. The Confederates offered terms providing that the Federals could take one boat and evacuate their remaining crews, but they would have to leave everything else. Since Commodore Renshaw was still out of action over on the disabled *Westfield*, a three-hour truce was agreed on to consider this remarkable demand.

Results/Impact

Leon Smith's choice to continue the attack and launch a third ramming attempt on *Harriet Lane* was almost certainly the most critical decision of the Battle of Galveston. Without it, the Confederates would have lost the battle. If Smith had withdrawn, the Union gunboats (including *Harriet Lane*) would have kept bombarding the city, and the Confederate artillery would have continued to be either destroyed or forced back from the waterfront. The Union fleet would have maintained its position in Galveston Harbor, and Magruder's desperate gamble on a nighttime attack using improvised gunboats and borrowed troops would have gone down in history as a complete disaster. Instead, by capturing *Harriet Lane* and using that vessel's guns to threaten (or bluff a threat against) the Federals, Smith eventually frightened what remained of the Union fleet out of Galveston Harbor. General Magruder's official report accurately praised Smith for his "indomitable energy and heroic daring," and gave him credit for defeating the enemy's fleet.[48]

Renshaw Blows Up Westfield *and Leaves Galveston Harbor*

Situation

Leon Smith's bold, outrageous demand that the Federal fleet surrender and use one vessel to transport all of the crew out of Galveston Harbor, leaving all of the remaining boats for the Confederates, should have been rejected out of hand. Yet it was not rejected because Commodore Renshaw, the officer who should have been confronted with it, was isolated on a sandbar in his flagship and had only limited knowledge of what was going on during the course of the battle. When he heard the remarkable nature of the surrender demand, and learned that one of his officers had agreed to a three-hour truce to consider it, Renshaw was livid. So far, Renshaw's night had gone about as badly as possible. But he still had one very important decision to make.

Options

Renshaw had three options. He could leave *Westfield* aground for the time being and direct what remained of his fleet to recapture *Harriet Lane* and drive off the Confederates from the city. The second option was that he could leave *Westfield* aground and take the rest of the ships out of Galveston Harbor to await a better opportunity to retake the city. The third possibility was that he could blow *Westfield* up to keep it out of Confederate hands and then take the remainder of the fleet out of the harbor.

Option 1

Renshaw could leave *Westfield* aground and transfer to another boat, where he could direct what remained of the fleet to recapture the *Lane* and drive off the Confederates. The commodore knew that Admiral Farragut would expect—indeed, demand—a course of action like that. Farragut had already warned him about the importance of making "a defense that will do credit to the Navy."[49] Nothing that had happened in the battle so far had done credit to the navy or anybody under the commodore's command. There was still a chance for Renshaw to turn the situation around.

Out on his sandbar, Renshaw did not know that the Confederate attack had largely exhausted itself. Magruder was beginning to withdraw his guns from the waterfront. Smith and his immobile collection of vessels were in no position to threaten anybody. The problem was that Commodore Renshaw was essentially making a decision in an information vacuum.

What Renshaw knew for certain was that the Confederates had stationed large artillery pieces along the waterfront and by now had captured the Massachusetts infantry (who had surrendered when the navy did not rescue them). He was aware that some enemy gunboats had somehow succeeded in capturing *Harriet Lane*, one of his most powerful gunboats. For all Renshaw knew, the strengthened Confederate fleet might now be preparing to move against what was left of his own, now significantly reduced, force. If he left *Westfield* intact and then was defeated or forced to flee, he might be leaving the enemy a powerful weapon to use against the navy. Losing two gunboats in one day would destroy Renshaw's reputation and would likely lead to serious formal charges.

Option 2

Renshaw could leave *Westfield* aground and take what remained of the fleet out of Galveston Harbor to await a better opportunity to recapture the city. With this choice, he could rapidly remove Federal ships from the harbor and

Attack of the Rebels upon Our Gunboat Flotilla at Galveston, Texas, January 1, 1863," depicting explosion of USS *Westfield* on the right. NH 59141. US Naval History and Heritage Command.

leave a chaotic and threatening situation behind. This was perhaps the easiest option, but it involved the most personal risk. Leaving *Westfield* to the enemy without any kind of fight risked censure and serious charges. Renshaw could defend the loss of *Harriet Lane* by noting that he had been unavoidably absent at the time of its capture. But leaving his own vessel intact for use by the Rebels was something that Admiral Farragut would never understand or forgive.

Option 3

Renshaw could blow *Westfield* up to keep it out of Confederate hands and then take the remainder of the fleet out of Galveston Harbor. Obviously, the commodore would prefer to keep his flagship intact, and he would like to wait for time and tide to give him a better opportunity to pull it free. But by this point it was daylight, and he feared the Confederates were preparing a renewed effort to seize *Westfield* and capture his stranded crew. As far as Renshaw could tell, things had gone very badly for the fleet during the battle. He was therefore reluctant to give the Confederates one more prize to boast about. Rigging explosives on *Westfield* would take some time, and it would not destroy the entire vessel and its contents. But blowing the vessel up would at least keep most of it out of enemy hands.

Decision

Renshaw decided to destroy *Westfield* and directed his remaining fleet to prepare to evacuate the harbor. At about 8:00 a.m., the commodore ordered two transports to come near his ship and take his crew on board. He selected an explosive charge and detonation device called a slow match to blow up *Westfield* and keep it out of Confederate hands. The decks were covered with turpentine, powder trails were laid to an open magazine filled with powder, and the safety valves on the boilers were chained shut to maximize the explosive power of the blast. Unfortunately, at about 8:45, the charge exploded prematurely, killing Renshaw and the crew of the small boat that was intended to carry him off.[50]

Results/Impact

Renshaw's destruction of *Westfield* and himself put a dramatic end to the Battle of Galveston. The commodore's disastrous decision to destroy and leave

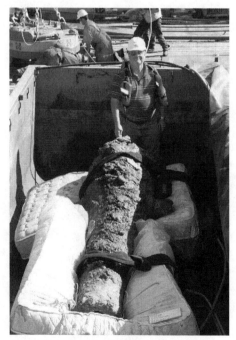

Author with the *Westfield*'s Nine-inch Dahlgren gun shortly after its salvage from the wreck in 2009. Author's collection.

meant that the Federals would attempt no coordinated plan that day to reverse the loss of *Harriet Lane*. It also meant that Galveston Harbor, the battlefield, would be abandoned to Magruder and his exuberant Confederates. What was left of the Union fleet then proceeded to evacuate Galveston Bay, still flying the white flags of truce. Capt. Richard Law, in command of *Clifton*, was Renshaw's successor in command by virtue of superior rank. It was not a desirable elevation in status. He was later successfully court-martialed for not attempting to recapture *Harriet Lane*. Farragut would later call the result of the battle the "most unfortunate" and the "most shameful" in the entire history of the US Navy.[51]

Renshaw's decision to blow up *Westfield* was not as effective as he might have hoped. On January 3, 1863, Magruder reported that the Confederates were busily salvaging the vessel's guns and armament. Fortunately for modern museumgoers, the Confederates were not completely successful in this endeavor. In 2009, the US Army Corps of Engineers organized the recovery of wreckage from the *Westfield* in advance of a major dredging operation planned for the Texas City Ship Channel. This project resulted in the largest archaeological salvage operation ever conducted in Texas waters. Over eight thousand artifacts were recovered and sent to the Conservation Research Laboratory at Texas A&M University. Although conservation was originally the main objective, the project grew into a major exhibit at the Texas City Museum. One of the items on display is one of *Westfield*'s nine-inch Dahlgren cannon, which somehow escaped Confederate salvage operations.[52]

CHAPTER 3

ONE DISASTER AFTER ANOTHER

The shocking Confederate victory at Galveston was followed by two Union disasters within three weeks that would solidify and extend that triumph. These disasters resulted from three critical decisions.

Farragut Sends Henry H. Bell to Recapture Galveston

Situation

On January 3, 1863, Maj. Gen. Nathaniel Banks and a staff officer were in New Orleans visiting Admiral Farragut on board his flagship, USS *Hartford*, when the admiral received the first telegram reporting that Galveston had been lost. The news was wildly inaccurate and sensational, claiming that an unspecified number of Confederate ironclads had materialized and caused the Union defeat. Perhaps remembering his angry refusal to allow Renshaw to withdraw, Farragut was greatly distressed about the battle's terrible outcome.[1]

The following day, when he received a more complete account of the fighting, Farragut reportedly was still depressed about the Galveston affair. Not only was the admiral's professional pride wounded, but he was worried by the Confederate capture of *Harriet Lane*, which he knew was one of the swiftest and most powerful gunboats in the Gulf. If the *Lane* was not promptly recaptured or destroyed, it might become a powerful weapon in the enemy's arsenal. Farragut knew that he could not waste any time ordering a relief expedition to Texas.[2]

In addition to General Banks, another important party was dining with Admiral Farragut when the bad news about Galveston arrived on January 3. Cmdre. Henry Haywood Bell was Farragut's close friend. Like the admiral, he was a Union naval officer from a Southern state (North Carolina). Both men were older and had enjoyed lengthy careers in the US Navy. Bell's pre-war service had involved lots of shore duty and fairly limited action. When the Civil War broke out, Bell was serving as ordnance officer in the West Point Foundry at Cold Springs, New York.[3]

In January 1862, Bell joined Farragut's West Gulf Blockading Squadron, where he became fleet captain. He then performed well, commanding a division of ships that forced their way past the lower Mississippi forts and helped Farragut capture New Orleans. Farragut trusted and respected Bell. In July 1862, with the admiral's support, Bell attained the rank of commodore. As 1863 approached, the two men were actively planning a campaign to attack and force the surrender of the forts at the entrance to Mobile Bay. The Galveston news suddenly halted that planning.[4]

When Farragut received the telegram notifying him of the events at Galveston, he was furious and ashamed. He immediately reported to Secretary of the Navy Gideon Welles what he knew about the battle, saying, "[It is] difficult to conceive a more pusillanimous surrender of a vessel to an enemy already in our power than occurred in the case of the *Harriet Lane*." He also vowed to send forces to Galveston immediately to recapture the city and the waters surrounding it. But whom should he send to accomplish this important task?[5]

Options

Farragut had two options with respect to the force sent to recapture Galveston: he could lead it himself, or he could appoint another officer to do so.

Option 1

Farragut could command the force himself. This would obviously be the admiral's first choice. As evidenced by his bold and risky strategy that resulted in the capture of New Orleans, he was aggressive by nature. Secretary Welles recorded in his diary that he believed Farragut would more willingly take great risks to obtain great results than any other high-ranking officer in military service. Although Farragut encouraged his subordinates to follow his example, the admiral knew that none of them would act as aggressively as he would if placed in a similar position.[6]

Farragut's son, Loyall, wrote a biography of his famous father in 1879. Loyall served as a clerk on Farragut's staff in late 1862 and was probably in the room when the admiral received the dreadful news about Galveston. In the chapter titled "Disaster at Galveston," Loyall recalled how chagrined his father was at hearing about the loss of the city. He "felt this misfortune deeply" because he saw it as undoing much of the good work that had been accomplished on the Texas coast. Loyall noted that his father's first impulse was to go to Galveston immediately. If he went there himself, Farragut knew that the situation would be handled quickly and appropriately.[7]

The problem with going to Galveston was that it meant putting everything else on hold until the admiral returned. This was a problem since there was so much going on elsewhere in Farragut's region of command. Plans were underway to capture Port Hudson, and operations were finally supporting the army's movements up the Mississippi River. It would be difficult for Farragut to direct these maneuvers remotely while actively directing a campaign at Galveston.[8]

The other problem with going himself was that Farragut's flagship, *Hartford*, had experienced great difficulty earlier in the war in crossing the sandbar at the entrance to the Mississippi River. At one point, the ship had been in peril of being lost while being pulled over the bar. Even if Farragut decided to go, it was not at all clear that *Hartford* could make the journey. He could transfer to another ship for the Galveston operation, but shifting the squadron's operations to a new vessel would take time and disrupt ongoing maneuvers.[9]

Option 2

Farragut could appoint another officer to lead the expedition to recapture Galveston. The advantage of this option was that the admiral could stay behind and continue to monitor operations elsewhere in the enormous territory of the West Gulf Blockading Squadron that he commanded. The problem with sending someone else to Galveston was that, as Secretary Welles correctly observed, no officer serving under Farragut's command would act as promptly and aggressively as the admiral himself. The admiral said on multiple occasions that his personal motto was acting with "celerity," a word meaning "speed and decisive movement." As Farragut was well aware, few of his key subordinates seemed to operate with the degree of urgency and determination he so strongly favored.[10]

Decision

Farragut decided to send his friend Cmdre. Henry H. Bell with a small fleet to retake Galveston. Although he was severely tempted to redeem the US Navy's

Cmdre. Henry H. Bell, USN, circa
1866. NH 56140. US Naval History
and Heritage Command.

honor himself, Farragut believed that the difficulty of getting *Hartford* over
the bar and the need for him to keep closely involved in operations elsewhere
meant that he could not spare the time to do so.

Farragut needed to quickly find a commander for the Texas operation, and
Bell was already present and up to speed on the Galveston debacle. Farragut
believed in the commodore's competence and zeal for the cause. Out of all his
subordinates, Farragut considered Bell the most appropriate person to repre-
sent him on the Texas coast.[11]

According to Bell's diary, shortly after hearing about the disaster at Galveston, he told Farragut that he was ready for any service. The admiral issued
written orders to Bell that same day to proceed to Galveston as soon as his
ship could sail. If Bell found conditions favorable, Farragut instructed him to
retake Galveston. If this was not possible, Bell was to send the gunboats up
into the harbor and retake or destroy *Harriet Lane*. The commodore was also
to use his gunboats to shell the Confederate troops out of any fortifications
they might be constructing. Although Farragut left the precise actions upon
reaching Galveston to Bell's good judgment, it was clear what the admiral
expected Bell to do. As it turned out, Bell would accomplish none of the tasks
assigned him.[12]

Results/Impact

Appointing Bell to lead the expedition to recapture Galveston was a mistake that almost certainly allowed the Confederates to maintain control of the city and Galveston Bay. Although Bell had told Farragut on January 3 that he was ready for any service, he was not ready for any service at all. He delayed leaving New Orleans until 11:00 a.m. the next day because, according to his diary, sixty of his men were still onshore engaging in activities of questionable morality. His vessel then experienced a series of mechanical problems, and it was not until 11:00 a.m. on January 7 that Bell finally reached Galveston. He then held off on attacking while waiting for additional ships to arrive. On January 9, Bell received a party of Confederate officers under a flag of truce and exchanged letters with General Magruder. The commodore noted in his diary that he gave his guests wine, cigars, and newspapers.[13]

While Bell delayed attacking, entertained Confederate officers, and waited for other ships to arrive, he could clearly see the enemy hard at work ashore throwing up breastworks and otherwise fortifying the city he was expected to capture. At 1:00 p.m. on January 10, Bell finally ordered two of his gunboats to throw a few shells at the working parties on the beach. He also launched a few shells over the island in an effort to strike *Harriet Lane* (whose masts he could see in the distance). The bombardment continued for about two hours with little result.[14]

Shortly after the firing stopped on January 10, nine days after the Confederates had recaptured Galveston, the steamer *Hatteras* arrived to complete Bell's force. Although the next day, January 11, dawned "clear and beautiful," Bell chose not to fire on the town during the morning because it was a Sunday. Unlike the Union fleet, the Confederates did not take Sunday off. Instead, Bell noted in his diary that he watched the enemy actively working on the fort on the point. The assistant paymaster on board USS *New London* vowed that when and if the bombardment was renewed it would be terrific, and that Galveston would then be a doomed town.[15]

Because of Bell's continued delay, Galveston would never be a doomed town. In fact, it was barely even threatened. Farragut wrote Bell on January 12 that he was sending him another ship, USS *Owasco*. With this addition to his force, Farragut was now quite assured that Bell had enough gunboats to recover Galveston. He even expressed his confident hope that *Owasco* was unnecessary because the city was already in Bell's possession. Farragut was wrong in both his hope and assumption. By January 12, five days after his arrival, Bell had accomplished absolutely nothing at Galveston.[16]

As he studied the situation on January 12, the same day that Farragut wrote him about *Owasco*, Bell was having cold feet about entering Galveston

Bay and recapturing the city. At about 4:00, he convened the commanders of all of his gunboats. Although the Confederates had strengthened the fort at the bay's entrance and there were potential issues finding the channel entrance without pilots, all the commanders indicated that they were willing and prepared to go into Galveston Bay and attack the city. Bell, however, was not convinced. He ultimately informed Farragut that he did not see any way to seize Galveston. In his diary Bell wrote, "There will be censure, inconsiderate censure, but I can't help it."[17]

By the time Bell held his conference of commanders on January 12, it was over eleven days since the Confederates had recaptured Galveston. Contrary to his instructions from Farragut, Bell had made no serious headway. While Farragut was assuring the secretary of the navy that Bell would swiftly restore Union control of Galveston, the commodore merely continued to blockade the entrance to the bay and watch the Confederates strengthen their defenses.

Farragut might have been right in his assessment that he could not just drop everything and head to Galveston himself. But he had chosen the wrong man for the job. Bell's delayed and timid approach allowed the Confederates critical time to fortify the city. These fortifications would be the key that kept Galveston in Confederate hands for the remainder of the war. Once the fortifications were complete, a direct assault on the city from the Gulf would be too difficult and costly to attempt. In early February, Bell reported to Farragut that the defenses had become too strong for the gunboats to overcome them. Union military planners recognized this reality and never again ordered a direct attack on Galveston after the fortifications were effectively complete.[18]

Alternate Decision/Scenario

Had Admiral Farragut of "damn the torpedoes" fame led the Galveston expedition in person, it is unimaginable that he would have acted as Bell did. He certainly would not have taken Sunday off and watched the Confederates fortify the area around the city without trying to prevent it. If Farragut had gone to Galveston himself, or if Bell had acted more boldly and decisively upon his arrival at Galveston, the gunboats might once again have forced their way into Galveston Harbor and captured the city. The city would almost certainly have surrendered when faced with the credible threat of its total destruction.

Magruder's battle plan on January 1 had succeeded in part because of its element of surprise and the fact that he had attacked at night. Neither of these elements would have been present had the Union gunboats attacked at a time of their choosing. Commodore Bell's flagship, the screw sloop *Brooklyn*, was much more powerful than any ship Renshaw had in Galveston Harbor on January 1. By itself, Brooklyn mounted a ten-inch gun and twenty-four nine-inch guns. If a spirited attack had been made, as Farragut expected, Magruder would probably have been forced to abandon Galveston. This would have prevented him from completing his defenses around the city, and Galveston would likely have stayed in Union hands for the remainder of the war.[19]

Instead of acting, Commodore Bell waited and pondered his next move. One of the key factors that led him not to attack Galveston was that on the evening of January 11, 1863, he lost *Hatteras*, the latest addition to his force, in a battle with the Confederate raider *Alabama*. If Bell had attacked Galveston on the afternoon of January 10 or the morning of January 11, however, the city would already have been in Union hands by the time that *Alabama* arrived.

Raphael Semmes Decides to Take CSS Alabama to Galveston

Situation

CSS *Alabama* started life as hull number 290 in the John Laird, Son & Company shipyard opposite Liverpool. On July 30, 1862, Confederate agents managed to sneak the vessel out to sea and narrowly avoided its seizure. In the Azores, the ship was united with its guns and crew and christened CSS *Alabama*. *Alabama*'s wheel was appropriately engraved with a motto in French that means "God helps those who help themselves." It has been accurately said that when launched, *Alabama* was probably the finest cruiser of its class in the world. Under the capable command of Capt. Raphael Semmes, it steamed from the Azores and began a career of commerce raiding on Union shipping that made headlines around the world.[20]

After leaving the Azores, Semmes directed his new cruiser to the New-foundland Banks, where he captured a dozen or more Union merchantmen. Semmes knew that when word of his raids got out, the Union would send powerful gunboats to chase him. Thus he could never stay in any particular area too long. As 1862 was drawing to a close, Semmes decided to find a new hunting ground and turned his vessel south and east. In the Caribbean, *Alabama* continued to capture more Union merchant ships, making them prizes or destroying them outright. So far, the thesis behind *Alabama*'s creation and mission as a commerce raider had been a tremendous success.[21]

Semmes was always alert to the news he could pick up from the crews of ships he captured. He also carefully noted the war news in captured newspapers. From them he learned of what the press called the Banks Expedition,

Photograph of Rear Adm. Raphael
Semmes, CSN. LC 2019637160.
Library of Congress.

supposedly an invasion force of between fifteen and thirty thousand men
heading for Texas. On December 7, 1862, near Cuba, Semmes intercepted
and captured the California mail steamer *Ariel*, which carried newspapers
from New York published as recently as December 1. Based on the newspaper
accounts, Semmes was convinced that the Banks Expedition was about to
reach Galveston, if it had not already done so. The captain knew from earlier
accounts that Galveston was then in Union hands, and reports suggested
that the expedition planned to leave the city for the Texas interior sometime
around January 10. Semmes had already determined to extend his raiding
territory to the Gulf of Mexico, but the potential presence of the Banks Expedition on the Texas coast presented him with a new opportunity. Was he
bold enough to seize it?

Options

Semmes had two options upon entering the Gulf of Mexico: he could continue raiding Union commercial shipping as he had been doing, or he could
head for Galveston and attempt to destroy some of the transports and supply
vessels expected to support the Banks Expedition.

<u>Option 1</u>

Semmes could continue disrupting the enemy's commercial shipping in the Gulf. That strategy had worked well for him so far. Commerce raiding in the Gulf would bring alarming new headlines in the North and drive up shipping insurance rates. In following this path and disrupting Northern commerce, Semmes would be doing what *Alabama* was designed to do. The problem with this "more of the same" approach was that Semmes believed *Alabama* was capable of doing even more. As a commerce raider, the captain could never control how many target vessels he might encounter or what their cargo might be. Also, though commerce raiding hurt the North economically by reducing international trade and making insurance more expensive, it did not directly affect Union military operations.

<u>Option 2</u>

Semmes believed he was potentially in position to strike a blow now that would directly disrupt a major Union initiative. Instead of waiting for more Union ships to come to him, he could go to Galveston, where he was reasonably certain a large number of ships would be located. If he timed his arrival just perfectly one evening, Semmes thought that he might be able to secretly approach the expedition's conglomeration of supply vessels from the rear and attack them.[22]

John Macintosh Kell, *Alabama*'s executive officer, considered this Semmes's boldest scheme. As the captain confided in him, the plan was to arrive after the Union fleet had anchored, when the provision ships would be carelessly moored together in deep water. In the night, *Alabama* could steam at full speed through them, pouring fire from both broadsides, sinking and burning ships as he passed. Semmes knew that if the operation worked out as he planned, it would arguably be the greatest naval accomplishment of the war for a single ship. If he passed on this opportunity, it might never come again.[23]

The problem with the strategy in Semmes's mind was that it was necessarily based on dated and incomplete information. He did not know the actual situation at Galveston. For all he knew, the Banks Expedition might not have arrived. There might be no transports or supply ships. There might only be Union warships eager and waiting to take him on. While these questions posed a substantial risk to his vessel and his crew, Semmes thought he had two advantages as he approached the Texas coast. First, *Alabama* had been designed for speed. It could make thirteen knots under steam and ten knots under sail, and the captain thought few Union blockaders or heavy gunboats could match that speed. The second advantage Semmes noted was that he possessed the element of surprise. The latest accounts in captured newspapers reported *Alabama* on its way down to Brazil. As far as Semmes could tell, nobody on the Texas coast had any reason to believe that he was within a thousand miles of Galveston.[24]

Decision

Despite his lack of current information, Semmes headed for Galveston to destroy some of the ships expected to accompany the Banks Expedition. Since the expedition was speculated to depart on January 10, Semmes set his course and speed to arrive off Galveston on the evening of January 11.

Results/Impact

Although almost all of Semmes's key assumptions were wrong, *Alabama*'s appearance made a major contribution to keeping Galveston in Confederate hands. Semmes knew that his understanding of the situation at Galveston might be inaccurate. He also knew that Union gunboats might be defending the transport fleet he expected to encounter. To minimize these risks, he planned to arrive just before nightfall on the eleventh, hoping to catch a distant glimpse of the enemy supply ships before hauling off and waiting for dark to make his grand assault. But he arrived off Galveston a little too early, and the lookout at the top of the mast did not spot the shore until too late.

When the lookout finally described the ships at the entrance to Galveston Bay, they turned out not to be the expected fleet of anchored supply ships. Instead, the lookout reported a significant number of enemy gunboats. To further confuse matters, the gunboats were firing a few lazy shells that burst ineffectively over the city. Semmes recorded his reaction in his memoirs: "There has been a change of programme here." Although he did not know of Magruder's surprising victory on New Year's Day, the captain quickly deduced that the Confederates must somehow have recaptured Galveston.[25]

As it turned out, the scenario that Semmes had expected was completely wrong. The only portion of the Banks Expedition that had reached Galveston was the small contingent of Massachusetts troops who had been captured ten days earlier in the Battle of Galveston. Semmes arrived on January 11 prepared to view a fleet of Union supply ships and instead was greeted by a fleet of Union warships. The captain later described his disappointed reaction: "Here was a damper!"[26]

Semmes could probably have turned out to sea immediately and gotten away without being observed, but he was reluctant to do so. Instead, he waited to see how the situation would develop. The captain had promised his crew that they would have some entertainment and serious action when they entered the Gulf of Mexico. Semmes and his men had made the long journey to the Texas coast, and he was not ready to retreat without seeing whether the situation allowed them to strike a blow for the Confederate cause.[27]

While Semmes was considering his options in light of the presence of active Union warships, the enemy helped make up his mind. A vigilant Federal lookout had spotted and reported a strange sail in the distance. As Semmes watched, a single vessel, USS *Hatteras*, pulled away from the Union fleet and headed in *Alabama*'s direction to investigate. "It was just the thing I wanted," the captain later recalled, "for I at once conceived the design of drawing this single ship of the enemy far enough away from the remainder of her fleet, to enable me to decide a battle with her before her consorts could come to her relief." By adjusting his speed, Semmes carefully lured *Hatteras* more than twenty miles out to sea.[28]

At about 7:00 p.m., *Alabama* opened the battle with a broadside and began a running exchange of fire with *Hatteras*. At some points, the ships were only about twenty-five yards apart, and men with small arms joined the battle. After about thirteen minutes, *Hatteras* had lost a number of its iron hull

Battle between USS *Hatteras* and CSS *Alabama* on January 11, 1863. Nineteenth-century print. NH 53690. US Naval History and Heritage Command.

plates, and its engine was disabled. The ship had begun to roll over, and its captain, Lieut. Cmdr. Homer C. Blake, had no alternative but to surrender. Ten minutes after Blake's crew was taken on board *Alabama*, *Hatteras* went down bow first. Semmes set sail for Jamaica with his prisoners. Commodore Bell would discover the wreck of the unfortunate *Hatteras* the next day.[29]

Hatteras would turn out to be one of the first iron-hulled warships sunk in combat. The waters off Galveston were the closest that CSS *Alabama* would ever come to a Confederate port. Even though Semmes had come to Galveston based on faulty information and a completely erroneous picture of the situation he would encounter, his fortuitous arrival and the sinking of the *Hatteras* very likely saved the city from being recaptured. As discussed above, the day after the sinking of *Hatteras*, Commodore Bell determined that it was too risky to even attempt to force his way into Galveston Harbor. One of the key reasons for his decision was that he had lost *Hatteras* to an unexpected enemy attack. Making matters worse, Bell did not know whether or when *Alabama* might return to again launch a surprise attack from behind. If Bell had been an overly cautious commander before the loss of *Hatteras*, now he was paralyzed.

Farragut was once more forced to send an apologetic account to Secretary Welles: "It becomes my painful duty to report still another disaster off Galveston." He noted that he had warned his subordinates all along the Gulf Coast to Florida to be on the lookout for the pirate *Alabama*. Admiral Farragut was greatly disheartened by the loss of *Hatteras* and the fact that it at least temporarily halted potential efforts to retake Galveston and redeem the navy's honor.[30]

Alternate Decision/Scenario

If Semmes had not directed the *Alabama* to Galveston and captured *Hatteras*, Commodore Bell would probably have succumbed to the pressure from his subordinates and the orders from Farragut and entered Galveston Harbor on January 12 or soon after. This would in all likelihood have resulted in the capture of the city. But *Alabama* happened to appear during the one brief window of time after Bell's arrival that would result in a key delay in such action.

After the Battle of Galveston on January 1, the Confederates were reported to be very busy throwing up earthworks and placing the guns of the *Westfield* and *Harriet Lane* in batteries.[31] By January 21, ten days following the *Hatteras* battle, Farragut told Secretary Welles that "he feared Bell had now missed his chance." It would not be impossible to retake Galveston, but as the spades filled with dirt on Galveston Island and fortifications were erected, the window for such action was clearly closing quickly.[32]

Magruder Launches Another Cottonclad Steamer Attack at Sabine Pass

Situation

Magruder had always known that if he recaptured Galveston, he would need to give his engineers time to complete extensive fortifications around the city. He had gotten lucky when *Alabama* appeared literally out of the blue on January 11 and sank the *Hatteras*. That had bought him some precious time, but it might not be enough by itself. If he wanted to complete his fortifications without hindrance, the general needed to create another major distraction nearby that would take some of the heat off Galveston and focus the enemy's attention elsewhere.

Magruder had come to Texas convinced that the best way to defend the state was to gain control of all the main bays and harbors. Sabine Pass was a natural line of defense because it lay between his Texas forces and the main enemy positions in Louisiana. Even before the battle started at Galveston, Magruder was considering a potential distraction involving Sabine Pass. The pass was located on the border between Texas and Louisiana, about sixty-two miles northeast of Galveston. The nature of the Union blockade there gave Magruder a unique opportunity to repeat his success at Galveston if he made another bold attack.

Options

Magruder had two options. He could launch another attack on the Union blockaders at Sabine Pass, or he could wait and see how events developed.

Option 1

Magruder could use cottonclad steamboats to assault Union blockaders at Sabine Pass. There were two river steamers, *Uncle Ben* and *Josiah H. Bell*, located on the Sabine River above Sabine Lake. It would not be too difficult to repeat what the Confederates had done at Galveston, lining the vessels' sides with cotton and placing some sharpshooters and artillery pieces on board.

If the right conditions materialized, these boats could steam out of the entrance to Sabine Pass and launch a surprise attack on the Union blockaders there. Observers reported that the blockaders at the pass were sailing ships and without steam engines. If the wind conditions were just right, the attacking steamers would have a substantial advantage because they could position themselves where the enemy's guns could not easily fire. Capturing or sinking the Union ships at Sabine Pass could be tremendously helpful to the Confederates. Not only would this free up another important Texas port for blockade-running and commercial traffic, it would also divert Union naval resources that might otherwise be directed at recapturing Galveston. If it succeeded, a Sabine Pass operation could be just the vital misdirection that Magruder so desperately needed.

However, this option might well fail. All of the advantages of the cottonclads were purely hypothetical. Although the boats had won the Battle of Galveston, one of them had sunk, and the artillery piece on the other had blown up and killed the gun crew. The two heavy cottonclads that would be used at Sabine Pass would not have much speed, and there could be no assurance that wind conditions or steam engine performance would give them much advantage over the blockaders. This was particularly true because the cottonclads were river steamers and had not been designed for speed or offshore travel. Launching a cottonclad attack on the open sea was risky, and this operation would occur in daylight without the cover of a shore bombardment. Magruder would certainly be taking a gamble if he gave the green light to this scheme.

Option 2

Magruder could hold off on an assault at Sabine Pass and see how events developed. He had just risked an enormous amount by attacking at Galveston. He had narrowly achieved a victory, but many elements of that plan had failed. The safest course of action, one that would appeal to most commanders, would be to stop additional attacks until the situation at Galveston had stabilized. The guns and men that would be required at Sabine Pass might be better put to use defending Galveston for the time being. Sabine Pass was a strategic position, but it was not nearly as important as Galveston. Putting the Sabine Pass action on hold would not mean its permanent cancellation. An attack at the pass using the two new boats could always be ordered in the future if it became necessary.

The problem with delaying this assault had to do with timing. Magruder did not know how much longer the Union would blockade Texas ports with sailing ships. There was already discussion in the navy about fixing that potential weakness. If Magruder intended to exploit the potential advantage of steam versus sail at Sabine Pass, he probably needed to do it soon.

The other crucial point was that Magruder needed the diversion of the proposed Sabine Pass operation now, when it could most benefit his construction activities at Galveston. The appearance of *Alabama* at Galveston had clearly paused Union plans to assault the city. But there was no way to know how long that pause might last. At any moment, Farragut might arrive with reinforcements, or Bell might suddenly realize that he held the advantage and summon up the nerve to enter the harbor. Magruder hoped that an attack at Sabine Pass, even if unsuccessful, might gain him further time to work on Galveston's fortifications as the navy dealt with yet another potential threat up the coast.

Decision

Magruder decided to launch another cottonclad attack at Sabine Pass. At 6:30 a.m. on January 21, 1863, the *Uncle Ben* and *Josiah H. Bell* steamed out of the entrance to Sabine Pass and headed toward the Union blockaders. The Federal blockaders consisted of USS *Morning Light*, with eight 32-pounders, and the schooner *Velocity*, which mounted only two small howitzers. As the Confederate vessels approached them, the Union ships made sail and attempted to withdraw out to sea.[33]

Results/Impact

Magruder's decision to launch the cottonclad attack at Sabine Pass had an even better outcome than he could have expected. After a chase of more than twenty miles, the winds calmed. The Confederate steamer *Josiah Bell* managed to approach the *Morning Light* from the rear, where the *Bell*'s rifled gun

"Capture of the U.S. Blockading Ship *Morning Light* off Sabine Pass, Jan. 21, 1863, by Rebel Copper [Cotton] Clad Boat *Uncle Ben*." Sketch by Francis H. Schell, 1863. The Miriam and Ira D. Wallach Division of Art, Prints and Photographs: Print Collection. New York Public Library. Retrieved from https://digitalcollections.nypl.org/items/6eaed3cc-75a9 -1df6-e040-e00a18065bf1.

could do serious damage without facing return fire. Eventually, the Confederates moved into even closer range, where their sharpshooters could sweep the Union ship's deck with deadly fire. After a running fight that lasted about two hours, the Union blockaders surrendered. Both ships were taken back to Sabine Pass. The *Morning Light* was eventually deemed too heavy to get over the sandbar at the entrance to the pass and was set afire and destroyed.[34]

Coming on the heels of the fall of Galveston and the sinking of the *Hatteras*, the loss of *Morning Light* and *Velocity* was a sharp disappointment for the Union and an equally sharp boost to Confederate morale. Even before he had received the report about the *Morning Light*, Farragut was already describing the events in Texas as the "severest blows of the war to the Navy." The loss of two more of his vessels to the enemy was a crowning blow.[35]

The string of Union disasters culminating in the capture of *Morning Light* had precisely the effect that Magruder had hoped. Bell ceased any pretense of hostile preparations at Galveston and instead sent two of his best commanders and gunboats to patrol the entrance to Sabine Pass. With the respite, Magruder improved his Galveston fortifications to the point where the Federals deemed them too strong to attack. A seriously depressed Farragut wrote to Commodore Bell on February 6, 1863, "Don't have any other disaster, if possible, for they are abusing us enough at home."[36] Bell got the message. While the spring and summer of 1863 proved very eventful elsewhere during the Civil War, there would be no serious campaigns or offensive operations on the Texas coast during that time.

CHAPTER 4

THE BATTLE OF SABINE PASS

The cascade of Union disasters in January 1863 led to a relatively easy time for Magruder and the Confederate forces in Texas for the next eight months. While important campaigns were being decided east of the Mississippi River, residents of the Lone Star State had the leisure to boast about their comparative success defending their own borders. As fall approached, however, it became increasingly likely that the Union would soon launch another invasion of Texas. But with the defenses of Galveston now greatly strengthened, where would such an invasion start? As it turned out, that location would be Sabine Pass, where the last of the three January disasters had occurred. The Battle of Sabine Pass, which took place on September 8, 1863, would be one of the more remarkable small battles of the Civil War. Six critical decisions made that engagement yet another Union disaster in Texas.

Lincoln Launches Another Expedition to Texas

Situation

After the fall of Vicksburg and Port Hudson on the Mississippi River, Union military planners had the opportunity to redirect their forces and open up another significant new front. Though they considered a number of options, eventually the choices boiled down to two. One involved an important target east of the Mississippi River; the other, a target that lay well to the west.

Pres. Abraham Lincoln, USA. Photograph
by Anthony Berger, 1864. LC-DIG-ppmsca-
19305. Library of Congress.

Since this decision was of such fundamental importance, and since the army
and the cabinet were divided in their opinions, President Lincoln himself was
called on to make the final choice in his role as commander in chief.

Options

President Lincoln could authorize an invasion of Alabama through Mobile or
authorize an invasion of Texas.

Option 1

Lincoln could authorize a campaign to invade Alabama through Mobile. Alabama was an appealing target for a variety of nonmilitary and military reasons. Its capital, Montgomery, was regarded in some circles as the "Cradle of
the Confederacy" because it had hosted the initial secession convention and
served as the rebellion's first capital. On the road to Montgomery, the first
prize in an Alabama campaign would be Mobile, which before the war had
been the second-largest cotton port in the South after New Orleans. After
the capture of the Crescent City in 1862, Mobile was the most important
Confederate port on the Gulf Coast and the second-largest Southern city by
population after Richmond.[1]

Mobile was also strategically important, standing near the top of a large bay that provided a convenient staging ground for an active fleet of blockade-runners. In addition, Mobile had access to two large navigable rivers and two principal railroads. The railroads were of particular importance because they linked the Alabama-Mississippi area of the war with the Georgia-Carolina area. They were also a critical supply line providing reinforcements, arms, and ordnance to Confederate armies fighting on battlefields to the north and east.[2]

Not only was Mobile of importance, but an invasion that began there could lead to the capture of the giant industrial machine that had evolved in central Alabama. Alabama possessed the best internal transportation network of waterways in the Confederacy. This enabled the state to produce and ship roughly 70 percent of the Confederacy's iron supply. Located on the Alabama River upstream from Mobile, Selma combined an enormous naval foundry, arsenal, and gunpowder supply facility. In size, Selma's foundry was second only to the Tredegar Iron Works in Richmond. It manufactured cannon as well as iron armor for warships. As an example of its capability, the *Tennessee*, the most powerful ironclad ever built by the Confederacy from the keel up, was produced in Selma.[3]

If the location to attack had been put to a vote by Union military leaders, Mobile would unquestionably have been the clear winner. There is simply no doubt that in 1863, Mobile and Alabama were more strategically important targets than Texas. Both Maj. Gen. U. S. Grant and Admiral Farragut strongly supported a Mobile operation. Farragut had said as early as December 1862 that he preferred an expedition against the city to any potential operation involving Texas. Grant had expressed a similar preference to his superiors. For once, Lincoln had his land and sea commanders on the same page supporting a critically important strategy and objective.[4]

The fact that Mobile was so clearly of military importance did not mean that a plan to capture it would necessarily succeed. There was a good reason why the city had not been attacked earlier in the war. By 1863, many military observers considered the military complex surrounding Mobile to be almost impregnable. Two enormous masonry fortifications guarded the entrance to Mobile Bay. Fort Morgan, the largest, had many heavy guns within almost point-blank range of the channel that a large warship would need to follow to enter the bay. It was also known that this channel was protected by torpedoes (floating mines). Successfully forcing a way in would take a determined commander like Farragut, many heavy Union warships, and a lot of luck. It would almost certainly result in many Union casualties.[5]

Even if the Federals could enter the bay, that was only the first part of the labyrinth. Mobile Bay shallowed substantially after the entrance, meaning that the large Union warships necessary to pass the forts could not get close enough to the city of Mobile to effectively bombard it. It would be up to the army, largely unsupported by the navy, to assault the city's formidable defenses. This would not be easy. By this point, Mobile was probably the best fortified city in the Confederacy and had been largely undamaged by the war. It had several continuous lines of earthworks, and the approaches were protected by batteries onshore, on islands, and even on floating platforms.[6]

It was all very well for bold commanders like Grant and Farragut to recommend an attack on Mobile, but Lincoln could see that an Alabama campaign would be lengthy. It almost certainly would be costly, and it might end up, as initial attacks on Vicksburg had, in defeat. This was not the sort of result that Lincoln needed going into the fall of 1863. He had just come off a string of triumphs at places like Vicksburg and Gettysburg. Did he really want to jeopardize that streak and authorize an operation that might be viewed as a disaster going into the 1864 election season?

The problem with not authorizing the Mobile campaign was that the operation would not get any easier if Union forces waited. As at Galveston, the Confederates at Mobile were constantly strengthening their defenses. Every day of waiting allowed them to potentially construct new earthworks, deploy more torpedoes, and build more ironclad rams. At some point, the Union would have to confront the Confederate military-industrial complex that began at Mobile. It was essential to concluding the war. Farragut and Grant were not alone in thinking that the sooner the operation was launched, the better its chances of success might be.

Option 2

Lincoln could authorize an invasion of Texas. Bringing the Lone Star State back into the Union would unquestionably be a major achievement. The biggest Confederate state by size, Texas furnished large numbers of extremely effective combat troops to Rebel armies outside its borders. Famous units like Walker's Texas Division and Hood's Texas Brigade were some of the most dependable troops in the western and eastern armies. If a Union expedition seized their homes, would these Texas soldiers continue to fight so fiercely, or would their morale instead be severely compromised? A Union campaign in one of the last largely unmolested areas of the Confederacy would answer that question.

There was also the question of how committed many Texans were to the Confederacy. Unionists had claimed for years that many loyal citizens remained in the state who were just waiting for the opportunity to join the country's cause if and when a sizable Federal force appeared. A good argument could be made that it was time to test this claim. A liberating force of soldiers might accomplish even more than rescuing these loyal citizens. Ever since the beginning of the war, influential New England governors had lobbied Lincoln to get control of a large cotton-growing region like Texas that could be separated from the rebelling South and used to supply cotton to idle textile mills. The *New York Times* published a series of editorials supporting the policy of carving out a safe cotton-supply area in Texas. If Lincoln played his cards right, the writers suggested, the state might even be brought back into the Union in time for its loyal and grateful citizens to vote in the 1864 presidential elections.[7]

Despite its surface appeal, there was a reason the Texas alternative was not a high priority for Lincoln's military advisers. A Texas operation did not have any of the readily apparent military advantages of an invasion of Alabama. There was no Selma equivalent in Texas that was supplying cannon or gunpowder to eastern battlefields. As far as Union military planners were concerned, Texas might as well have been an island. Located well west of the Mississippi River, it was not directly connected by rail or navigable waterway to the remainder of the Confederacy. In fact, with the fall of Vicksburg, it was difficult for Texans to find a way to supply men or materiel to armies fighting east of the river.

Even if Lincoln launched an expedition to Texas, he knew that it might be difficult to occupy and subdue the state. Its vast expanse and few natural supply lines made any campaign in the interior logistically challenging. Texans had shown in January 1863 that they were remarkably creative and willing to defend their coastal positions with extreme vigor. An invasion force into Texas might not require the enormous land and sea resources necessary to capture Mobile, but military planners in Washington were all too familiar with the danger of underestimating Texas resistance.

If the factors noted above were all that needed to be weighed, Lincoln would probably have had an easy time trusting the judgment of his military advisers and targeting Mobile. But there was one final concern, having nothing to do with military or economic considerations, that made Lincoln's decision very difficult. Texas's long border with Mexico, a foreign state, made it different from all the other Confederate states.

While the United States was distracted by war, France had used the instability in Mexico and a debt position to exert influence over the Mexican government. On June 10, 1863, a French army captured Mexico City. On July 11, an assembly chosen by the French proclaimed that Mexico would become an empire. French emperor Napoleon III had already settled on a plot in which Archduke Maximilian and his wife, Charlotte, would become the emperor and empress of this new monarchy.[8]

President Lincoln and his cabinet officials were greatly concerned by the French intervention. They had attempted to dissuade France and other European powers from taking control of Mexico. Secretary of State William Seward had even taken the extraordinary step of drafting a letter forwarded to Maximilian urging him not to take the crown, because the United States could only support a republican system of government in its southern neighbor. None of these entreaties were successful, however, and French plans to create an unfriendly monarchy in Mexico continued to progress.[9]

Lincoln and Seward had good reasons to distrust French designs in Mexico. France had opposed the American annexation of Texas, and it was widely believed that some elements in the French government were eager to see an independent Texas or a French protectorate emerge from the chaos of the Civil War. The new Republic of Texas, the French hoped, might serve as a stable source of cotton to Europe and conveniently provide a buffer between French-controlled Mexico and the remainder of the country.[10]

A letter written to the Confederate governor of Texas by a French consular official in Galveston in August 1862 seemingly confirmed France's interest in the reestablishment of the Republic of Texas. A copy of the letter had fallen into Union hands and was printed in Northern newspapers in January 1863. This news greatly alarmed many Northerners, and some began openly advocating a war with the meddling French. Others urged the Lincoln administration to take immediate action to seize and protect Texas.[11]

The last thing Lincoln needed in the summer of 1863 was to be forced into a war with Mexico. But he also did not want to go down in history as the American president who lost the largest state in the Union to a foreign power. Secretary Seward and other prominent officials urged him to order a show of strength in Texas as soon as it could be arranged.

Decision

Lincoln ordered the military to firmly plant the United States flag in Texas soil as soon as possible. He wrote a conciliatory letter to Grant explaining that he saw the military advantages of a campaign against Mobile, but that in view of recent events in Mexico, the Texas campaign simply must take priority.[12] It is important to note that at this stage in the planning, Lincoln did not specify any particular place where the expedition would begin. He merely put in motion a show of strength in Texas that he hoped would deter any action by the French.

Results/Impact

Lincoln's decision to prioritize the Texas campaign led directly to a series of unsuccessful operations to secure a significant Union foothold in the state. The first such campaign would begin and end with the Battle of Sabine Pass (September 8, 1863). That battle would not have been fought without Lincoln's decision to target Texas. All of the threats to Galveston and other places in Texas that continued through 1864 resulted from Lincoln's choice in the summer of 1863 to postpone the Alabama campaign and continually prioritize asserting Union authority in Texas.

Alternative Decisions/Scenario

If Lincoln had done as his generals and admirals suggested and put his resources solidly behind invading Alabama in 1863, such a campaign might have been successful and made a significant contribution to the war effort.

The military advantages from invading Alabama were quite real, and capturing that state earlier might have significantly weakened the Confederacy and its critical military and industrial resources at a key point in the war. The difficulty in evaluating whether such a campaign might have succeeded in 1863 lies in the realities of available resources. In the fall of that year, commanders like Grant, Sheridan, and Farragut were otherwise occupied. As shown hereafter, Confederate success at the Battle of Sabine Pass would eventually owe much to the errors of Union generals like Nathaniel Banks, who planned the campaign, and William B. Franklin, who was in charge of carrying out the plan. The naval resources assigned to the Texas operation were similarly reduced both in competence and capability. If these same officers and forces had been thrown at an even more difficult objective such as Mobile, it is difficult to see how they could have succeeded.

One other possible scenario may be worth considering. Had Lincoln put all his resources behind an Alabama campaign, might the French have been so emboldened that they actually tried to fill the vacuum in Texas, launching some covert scheme to separate it as an independent republic? It is questionable whether such a scheme could have succeeded, but it is certainly not outside the realm of possibility. It is certainly true that the French saw such a result as greatly to their advantage and internally discussed ways to facilitate a separation. Indeed, General Grant was so concerned about plans of this sort that near the end of the war in 1865 he directed large numbers of troops to the Rio Grande to guard against them.[13]

General Banks Orders an Invasion to Begin at Sabine Pass

Situation

Lincoln had ordered an operation to plant the Union flag firmly in Texas, but he did not specify exactly where he wanted the flag planted. Although he mentioned "western Texas" in his letter to Grant, there is no indication that the generals in charge of implementing the operation confined themselves to any particular objective.

The Texas coastline is approximately 367 miles long if a line is drawn from point to point, and approximately 3,359 miles if the measurement accounts for the actual length of all of the winding coastal boundaries. This second measurement (called Method 2 in federal data sources) is so different because the Texas coast includes numerous bays, islands, estuaries, and passes.[14] By the fall of 1863, the Union navy had attempted operations at many of the largest of these coastal zones. These efforts had been generally unsuccessful, and some, as at Galveston, had been outright disasters.

There was a great deal of controversy about where the newly authorized Texas operation should commence. General-in-Chief Henry Halleck at first thought that the best landing spot was Galveston. He then warmed to the idea of another less contested position farther down the coast like Indianola. The mercurial Halleck then changed his mind and expressed enthusiasm for a long looping movement up the Red River through Louisiana that would also strike westward into the heart of east Texas. Why did he not settle on one objective? It is apparent that Halleck knew the unfortunate history of operations in Texas and did not want to take the blame if this one failed. Fortunately, he could delegate the starting-point decision to a blameworthy subordinate.[15]

Maj. Gen. Nathaniel P. Banks had been sent to New Orleans in December 1862 to take command of the Department of the Gulf. A former Massachusetts governor, Banks had shown little ability as an army commander. His transfer to the Southwest owed primarily to Lincoln's hope that he might be more successful in an administrative capacity. Banks had commanded the department for only a few weeks before the Battle of Galveston handed him his first Texas disaster. In plotting the army's return to Texas nine months later, Banks undoubtedly wanted to redeem his rather tarnished reputation.[16]

President Lincoln wrote Banks directly on August 5, 1863, telling him that recent events in Mexico made early action in Texas more important than ever. The following day, Halleck instructed Banks to restore the flag to some point in Texas with the least possible delay. Without directly mentioning the French or Mexico, Halleck made it clear that the movement to Texas needed

Maj. Gen. Nathaniel P. Banks,
USA. Photograph by Matthew
Brady. LC-USZ62-119420.
Library of Congress.

to take place as soon as possible. Although Halleck had previously suggested a number of locations for potential operations, in this authorization of the new Texas campaign, he did not direct Banks to land at any particular place.[17]

Four days later, Halleck gave Banks more detailed instructions. Noting that the Texas operation was necessitated by diplomatic rather than military considerations, Halleck said that the most important goal was raising the flag in Texas where it could be sustained. Telling Banks again that he could select any place for occupation and that the choice was entirely his own, Halleck now expressly advised against an attack at Indianola or Galveston. He instead reiterated the wisdom of a movement up the Red River. Once more, Halleck stressed that this proposed Louisiana movement was merely his own suggestion and not a military instruction.[18]

As ordered, Banks began urgent preparations to send a large invasion force to Texas. Due to the limited number of suitable transports, the first wave would involve around five thousand soldiers. The general anticipated that subsequent waves would eventually swell the force to three or four times that number. Banks knew that a large body of troops is most vulnerable when it is first attempting to land in enemy territory. For this reason, he understood that his choice of a landing spot would be absolutely critical.

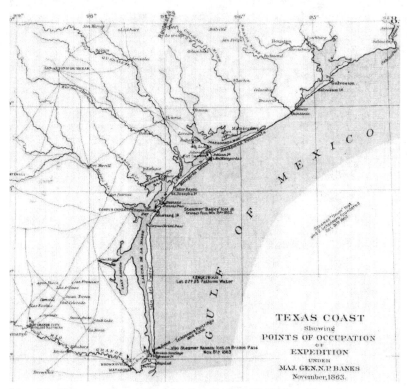

Map of the Texas coast prepared for Maj. Gen. Nathaniel P. Banks in November 1863 showing potential points of Federal occupation. Plate 43, *Atlas to Accompany the Official Records of the Union and Confederate Armies in the War of the Rebellion.*

Options

Banks considered five places to begin his Texas expedition. He could land (1) in south Texas near the Rio Grande, (2) at Indianola, (3) at Galveston, (4) at Sabine Pass, or (5) in northeast Texas after ascending the Red River in Louisiana.

Option 1

Banks could start the expedition in south Texas near the Rio Grande. Halleck had not specifically told Banks of Lincoln's fears about the French in Mexico, but Halleck's references to diplomatic considerations and European complications hinted strongly that these elements were behind the Texas movement.

Lincoln had also told Banks informally that Texas had become a priority because of unspecified events in Mexico. If the issue was countering potential French activities, Banks knew that landing troops near the Mexican border made a great deal of sense. It would deter any potential invasion attempt and be a strong show of force at an appropriate location.

The problem with a landing near the Rio Grande was that the starting point would be hundreds of miles from the main habitations and commercial hub of Texas. Planting the Union flag on a south Texas beach made no real contribution to the war effort. To get anywhere more important would not be easy. Moving up the coast of Texas from its tip would involve marching hundreds of miles over a series of long barrier islands that provided little in the way of roads, food, water, or shelter. It would be extremely difficult to move a large force up the coast, and the difficulties associated with supplying those troops would be enormous. Banks also anticipated that Magruder and his resourceful Confederates would find a way to contest every important river crossing on his march up the Texas coast.

In a communication on August 28, 1863, Halleck advised Banks to be very cautious in moving toward the Rio Grande. If Magruder and Kirby Smith combined their armies, Halleck warned, they could isolate a Union force in south Texas and give it much trouble. If he was uncertain before, by now Banks knew that Lincoln and Halleck were simply not operating on the same page concerning what they wanted him to do in Texas and where they wanted him to do it.[19]

Option 2

Banks could begin his expedition at Indianola, a port near the entrance to Matagorda Bay. It was centrally located on the Texas coast and much closer to San Antonio and Austin than many of the other options. Indianola had originally been suggested to Halleck by Secretary of the Navy Welles, who thought it was close enough to the Rio Grande to deter invasion and close enough to the main part of Texas to be strategically relevant. Unlike some other potential locations, Indianola was conveniently located on a bay that would admit at least shallow-draft vessels. The port was also inhabited by a number of loyal citizens of German origin.[20]

One problem with Indianola was that hardly anybody in the North had ever heard of it. It was a small town (today a ghost town) that had only a small dock and no material railroad connections. It earned its primary fame before the war in 1856–57, when Jefferson Davis, then the secretary of war, landed two shiploads of camels there in a failed experiment to find a new method of transporting military supplies in arid regions.[21]

The other problem with Indianola was the strong presence of Confederate artillery in the area. Farther up Matagorda Bay from Indianola was the town of Port Lavaca. From October 31 to November 1, 1862, well-disciplined Confederate gunners had exchanged bombardments with two Union gunboats in what became known as the Battle of Port Lavaca. That battle had ended when a large gun on *Westfield* exploded, and the Union vessels withdrew.[22]

Even if Banks could overcome the Confederate forces around Matagorda Bay, he learned that Halleck had changed his mind and now expressly advised against a landing at Indianola. Although he had almost immediately qualified that statement by leaving the decision entirely to Banks, no general would have been comfortable choosing a landing spot that his superior had expressly warned against.

Option 3

Banks could choose to land at Galveston. Although Halleck had expressly advised against this destination, Banks knew that taking Galveston and the railroad network around Houston would go a long way toward rebuilding his military reputation. This was still the most important part of Texas, and Banks knew that its capture would give the Union effective control of the state's major resources. Galveston's fall would be front page news in every Northern newspaper. It also would have important results. Banks had previously assured Halleck that if they could only find a way to take Galveston, the rebellion in Texas and neighboring Louisiana would fail.[23]

The problem with assaulting Galveston was that by the summer of 1863, Magruder and his forces had completed an elaborate set of fortifications around the city and the entrances to Galveston Bay. Banks had been advised that these defenses were too extensive and strong to be directly attacked. There had already been too many Union disasters in and around Galveston, and Banks was understandably reluctant to take a chance on adding to that number. A direct assault at Galveston involved high risks but also a high potential reward. Banks would love to take the city, but only if he could find a relatively safe way to do it.[24]

Option 4

Banks could land the expedition at Sabine City, which was located on the Texas side of the entrance to Sabine Pass. In all the communications involving Lincoln, Banks, and Halleck, Sabine Pass had never been mentioned as a potential landing spot. As far as Banks was concerned, that was a strong positive. Halleck had not advised against it, and its location on the border with Louisiana gave it at least some connection with the Red River / East Texas strategy that seemed to be Halleck's latest fancy. It also appealed to Banks that the waters between Sabine Pass and his supply base at New Orleans were largely under Union control.[25]

Disembarking at Sabine Pass was certainly not ideal from the standpoint of planting the flag where it would deter the French from crossing the Rio Grande. In fact, the pass was about as far from the Rio Grande as it was possible to get. But the instructions that Banks had received merely required him to raise the Union flag somewhere in Texas. Banks did not fool himself into believing that a landing at the pass was important in itself. However, it might provide access to other more strategic points in the interior.

The railroad network extending from Houston passed east through Beaumont and reached the Sabine River at the Louisiana border. This was not too far north of Sabine Pass. A landing at the pass might enable Union forces to march up to the railroad and use it as a route to proceed west and capture Houston. The city was not fortified to any significant degree. With Houston and the rail network under Union control, Galveston could be cut off from the mainland and taken by siege with relatively little difficulty. If everything worked out, landfall at Sabine Pass offered the potential of a relatively un-contested landing and a convenient line of march and supply, as well as the possibility of quickly achieving the military and commercial objectives of a Texas campaign.

The problem with a landing at Sabine Pass was that Banks did not know much about Confederate fortifications and forces in the area. He knew that cottonclad gunboats had been operating in the vicinity, and that those vessels had come out and captured the *Morning Light* earlier in the year. He was also aware of the Confederate fort at the entrance to the pass. All Banks knew about Sabine Pass was that a Union gunboat had captured a previous fort near there fairly easily in late 1862. The primary risk of sending a large invasion force to Sabine Pass was that his troops would be in a landing area that was likely contested and not well scouted. Banks certainly had almost no recent information about what he would face at this destination.

Option 5

Banks could launch an assault up the Red River in Louisiana and then cross into Texas. This was the latest plan that Halleck had suggested, and it appeared to be one of his favorites. It involved the army and navy advancing up the Red River to Alexandria and moving against Shreveport. From there the army would eventually proceed west into the northeast part of Texas. Banks knew that Halleck strongly approved of this Red River operation. Indeed, it was something of a fixation with Halleck. If the scheme succeeded, the campaign would capture an important cotton-producing region and cut off Confederate forces in Texas from those in Louisiana. It would also result in the capture of Shreveport, the headquarters of the Confederate Department of the Trans-Mississippi and the capital of Confederate Louisiana.

One problem with a potential Red River operation was that it seemed overly ambitious. As later events would substantiate, a combined operation that involved a lengthy movement up a river system surrounded by enemy troops was inherently difficult. To Banks, a surprise landing somewhere on the Texas coast followed by a standard infantry campaign seemed much simpler to put in motion.

Another difficulty with the Red River plan was that it didn't really seem to accomplish President Lincoln's original objective. Banks had been repeatedly instructed to plant the Union flag in Texas as soon as possible. The purpose of doing so was to deter the French from crossing the Rio Grande. Launching a massive operation up the Red River in Louisiana that might lead to the flag flying in some distant place in the northeast corner of Texas involved a lot of marching and a lot of time. It clearly was not the quickest or the most direct way of achieving Banks's goal.[26]

Decision

Banks initiated his Texas expedition with a landing at Sabine Pass. As he later explained to President Lincoln, Banks believed that a landing there would be relatively simple since the pass was on the eastern end of the Texas coast, relatively close to New Orleans. He also believed, based on the best information he had, that the Federals would encounter no serious resistance. After disembarking at Sabine City, the force was to march the relatively short distance north to the railroad line and then continue west toward Houston. Banks would later justify his decision by claiming that except for events outside his control, his plan would have placed twenty thousand soldiers in Houston within ten days after landfall.[27]

Results/Impact

The decision to land at Sabine Pass proved to be a mistake, and it was a significant cause of the Union defeat at the resulting battle. Of all the places to start the expedition in Texas, Sabine Pass was perhaps the worst choice. Although he did not know it, Banks had ordered his troops in Texas to sail directly into a trap. This was in large part a consequence of geography. Large transports and warships had difficulty getting over the sandbar at the entrance to Sabine Pass. By definition, the types of shallow-draft gunboats that

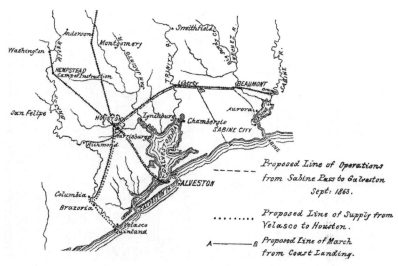

Map sent to President Lincoln by Major General Banks showing Union plan of operations from Sabine Pass to Galveston. *Official Records of the Union and Confederate Armies in the War of the Rebellion*, volume 26 (part 1).

were light enough to enter the pass could not be heavily armored. Once they entered the pass, they would then be funneled into narrow channels that exposed them to plunging artillery fire from the Confederate fort directly ahead of them. This was a fatal combination.

Although Banks didn't really know what his men would face at Sabine Pass, he was confident in their overwhelming advantage over the Confederate defenders in numbers of men and guns. His assumption was correct. The problem was that the artillerymen in the fort could direct their fire against him from strategically located positions, while his own position on moving transports and gunboats operating in narrow channels prevented him from responding with his full force. Some Union observers accurately characterized the Confederates in the fort as treating the battle like they were shooting fish in a barrel. Although Banks would later defend his decision as making the best of a bad situation, the truth is that he blundered badly by sending all his fish into the Sabine Pass barrel.

Confederate Engineers Decide to Relocate and Strengthen the Fort at Sabine Pass

Situation

At the beginning of the war, the Confederates hastily erected Fort Sabine near the entrance to Sabine Pass. Even for the time, it was not a modern fortification; it was instead an irregular mound of dirt in the shape of a half-moon. At its highest point the fort stood about ten feet high. The only guns in it were old and in bad condition. Badly designed and badly positioned, Fort Sabine was easily captured by Union gunboats in September 1862. This capture was made easier by the fact that the Confederate garrison had been severely depleted by yellow fever. With no Union infantry forces to occupy it, the fort soon fell back into Confederate hands.[28]

Even before Magruder's arrival in Texas, it was apparent that something needed to be done about Fort Sabine. Julius G. Kellersberg, a talented engineer from Switzerland, surveyed the stronghold and determined that it was too low and not appropriately designed to take advantage of its position along the narrow channels of the pass. When General Magruder arrived in Texas, Kellersberg urged him to do something about this dilapidated fort.[29]

After the Battle of Galveston, Magruder and his engineers were entirely occupied for a few months supervising the construction of elaborate fortifications around the city. By spring, however, with Galveston's fortifications in satisfactory condition, the issue of defenses at Sabine Pass resurfaced. It was time to make an important decision.[30]

Options

General Magruder had three options. He could leave Fort Sabine as it was, strengthen it in its current position, or build a new fort at a different location.

Option 1

Magruder could leave the fort as it was. With the Confederates' limited resources, this would seem an attractive option. Sabine Pass had never been deemed a port of tremendous strategic importance. As events had developed so far, both sides regarded the Galveston/Houston region and other areas on the Texas coast to be of far greater military and economic significance. Magruder had no reason to think that Sabine Pass was of particular interest to the Union. After all, when it had been captured in 1862, the Union had done nothing of consequence there and had soon chosen to abandon the fort.

Doing something about the fortifications at Sabine Pass meant spending scarce military resources that might be better employed elsewhere. The problem with doing nothing, however, was that the Union might find a way to again enter Sabine Pass and go north into east Texas, or find a way to circle around to the west and threaten Houston. In addition, the pass had become a convenient avenue for blockade-runners to reach international markets and supplement the war effort. If the Union gained control of the pass, all blockade-running through it would grind to a sudden halt. Magruder believed that it was important to make at least a show of defending Sabine Pass. This was why he had authorized the cottonclad expedition that captured the *Morning Light* in January 1863.

Option 2

Magruder could strengthen the fort at its current location. Although his European engineers did not like the primitive design of Fort Sabine, there was nothing fundamentally wrong with the structure that could not be fixed with some carefully supervised labor. Walls needed to be moved and the whole fort raised, but these tasks could be accomplished without building an entirely new stronghold elsewhere. However, reinforcing the existing fort would still leave it too close to the entrance of the pass. This location meant that Fort Sabine could be easily bombarded by larger ships situated in deeper water outside Sabine Pass.

In addition, authorizing any major fort construction activity at Sabine Pass would require massive amounts of labor, and this was potentially a problem. Thousands of enslaved people had been imported from the cotton plantation regions that served Galveston to build the fortifications there. But Jefferson County, where Sabine Pass was located, was one of the areas in the state where enslaved people were not very plentiful. It would be difficult to assemble and then transport a suitable labor force to the pass.[31]

Option 3

Magruder could build a new fort at a new location. Col. William H. Griffin, a former West Point–trained engineer who was in charge of the infantry at Sabine Pass, had suggested a potential new position for the stronghold. This spot was farther from the entrance to the pass and located on a small point jutting into the waters of the pass. The point was strategically located near the top of an oystershell reef. This reef was important because it created two channels, a Texas channel on the west and a Louisiana channel on the east.[32]

Griffin's proposed fort location on the point was ideal from an engineering perspective. Using a classic European design, Magruder's engineers proposed that the new structure have a triangular footprint. It would be on higher ground than the old one, and its guns would therefore possess a higher elevation. All of these features argued strongly in favor of the new fort location and design.

The problem with a new location and design was that it would require massive amounts of imported labor to build the fort, move in its guns, and then put the fort back in working order. This work would necessarily take place during the summer and would potentially subject the laborers and the garrison to the ravages of yellow fever. If the Union forces arrived during the transitional period when the fort was being relocated, the operation might even make Sabine Pass more vulnerable.

Decision

Magruder decided to erect a new fort at a new location. Since Colonel Griffin had suggested the site on the projecting point, the new structure was eventually named "Fort Griffin" in his honor. Fort Griffin's design took maximum advantage of its location. It featured six guns situated so that each had a field of fire straight down the channels, with the option of pivoting the guns to the side as ships passed. Thus the fort's guns would be firing from directly ahead of gunboats coming up the channels. This would limit the guns that could be fired at the fort to those located near the bow or front-deck area of attacking vessels.[33]

Results/Impact

The Battle of Sabine Pass ended in a Confederate victory when the two leading Union gunboats were disabled by highly accurate fire from Fort Griffin. The location and design of that fort turned out to be absolutely critical to the outcome of the fighting. It was far enough from the entrance to the pass that the Union gunboats could not simply bombard it into submission with their broadside guns. The fort was situated so that gunboats would have to enter the pass and approach up the narrow channels directly into its concentrated field of fire. This also meant that the approaching gunboats could fire only a fraction of their guns in response.

The position and design of the new stronghold made all the difference. If Fort Sabine had been left as it was, the battle would likely have ended as a quick Union victory. Even if Fort Sabine had been subjected to a substantial upgrade, it might have held out a little longer. But its location would not have allowed the fort's garrison to funnel the enemy into channels where the Confederates had such a dramatic advantage in terms of fields of fire.

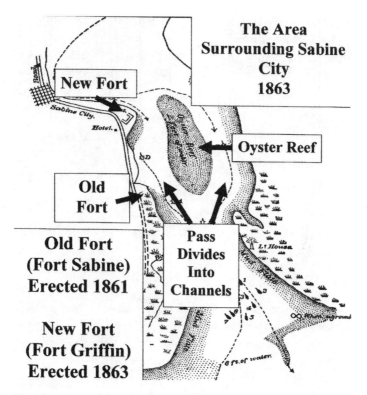

The Area Surrounding Sabine City 1863

New Fort

Oyster Reef

Old Fort

Old Fort (Fort Sabine) Erected 1861

Pass Divides Into Channels

New Fort (Fort Griffin) Erected 1863

Map of entrance to Sabine Pass from *Official Records of the Union and Confederate Armies in the War of the Rebellion*, volume 26 (part 1), with author's notes about relocation of fort.

Fort Griffin's location and design made Confederate victory possible at the Battle of Sabine Pass and were key factors in the outcome of the campaign. If Union forces had landed at the pass, it is highly likely that they might have continued on to capture Houston and Galveston as General Banks planned.

Commodore Bell Decides to Change the Navy's Role

Situation

Once Banks commenced his plan to capture Houston and Galveston by way of a march from the Sabine Pass area, he turned to the navy for support. Admiral Farragut had left for New York in early August. His temporary replacement in command of the West Gulf Blockading Squadron was Cmdre. Henry Bell, who was still smarting from his failure to recapture Galveston earlier in the year. Bell was delighted to hear of Banks's plan to invade Texas. He undoubtedly saw this as just the chance he was looking for to redeem his and the navy's reputation.[34]

Options

Bell and Banks had two options in designing the joint attack on the Confederate position at Sabine Pass. The offensive could be primarily an army operation with which the navy cooperated, or it could be primarily a navy operation with which the army cooperated. The difference was more than semantic. The first option would subject the fort to a direct infantry assault and possibly a siege. The second option would put the navy's gunboats at primary risk in a direct engagement with the fort.

Option 1

The attack on Sabine Pass could be primarily an army operation with which the navy cooperated. This was, in fact, the original plan. In ordering Banks to plant the flag in Texas, Halleck had assumed a movement by the army with which the navy merely collaborated. As originally sketched out by General Banks, the Sabine Pass operation was to involve mainly the army's landing and subsequent assault on the Confederate fort. The navy was being invited only to provide some covering fire and help screen the landings.

Banks knew that if the army successfully assaulted the Confederate fort through a movement on land, it would receive the primary credit. However, if the navy's gunboats managed to subdue the fort, the navy would justifiably be entitled to the credit. There was more than army-navy rivalry at stake in the design of the attack. If the army managed to land a significant force, Banks knew these soldiers would heavily outnumber whatever small garrison was in the Confederate fort. But to capture the enemy's stronghold they would then have to approach it over open ground. In this case, Banks had to assume that the attackers would take heavy casualties from guns firing antipersonnel ammunition such as canister. If the navy's gunboats were kept at a distance in a reserve role, the guns on those vessels were unlikely to make much of a difference.

Option 2

The attack on Sabine Pass could be primarily a naval operation with which the army cooperated. Banks and Bell had communicated with Act. Vol.

Lieut. Frederick Crocker, the officer in charge of the September 1862 action that captured Fort Sabine. Crocker did not have current information about the defenses at Sabine Pass, but he expressed confidence that the gunboats could again easily force the new fort's garrison to leave or surrender.[35]

Crocker's confidence was not mere bluster. Earlier in the year, he had led a similar gunboat attack on Fort Burton in Louisiana and captured it. Bell had faith in Crocker. After surveying his fleet, Bell chose four shallow-draft gunboats, including Crocker's own vessel, *Clifton*, that he believed could achieve the same result at Sabine Pass. If the attack succeeded, as Crocker assured him it would, the navy would get substantial credit, and the army would avoid the casualties from a direct assault on the fort.[36]

The problem with placing the gunboats at the front of the attack was that neither Bell nor Banks understood what situation the vessels would encounter. Bell knew from Crocker's 1862 experience that there were probably two old 32-pounder guns in the Confederate fort. However, none of the planners of this expedition had any information about the size or quantity of other guns in the fort. This was not trivial information. There was some light iron armor protecting the machinery and engines on *Clifton*, but it would provide little protection against artillery. As proved by a prior engagement at Vicksburg, *Clifton* was uniquely vulnerable to plunging fire from batteries situated straight ahead of it. Sending lightly armored vessels into an engagement with artillery positions, particularly given the narrow channels at Sabine Pass, would be a major risk.[37]

Decision

Commodore Bell met with Maj. Gen. William B. Franklin, who would be heading up the Sabine Pass operation for the army. They jointly agreed that Captain Crocker and the navy's four shallow-draft gunboats would make the initial attack on the fort alone. The force would be supplemented by 180 sharpshooters from the army divided among the four vessels.[38]

Results/Impact

Having the gunboats lead the assault on Fort Griffin proved disastrous and led directly to Union defeat. The plan agreed on before the expedition left New Orleans was to have the gunboats launch a surprise attack at dawn on September 7, 1863. However, a variety of mistakes eliminated the element of surprise and delayed the movement until the afternoon of the following day. Shortly after 4:00 p.m. on September 8, the gunboats weighed anchor and began their attack. *Sachem* and *Arizona* steamed up the Louisiana channel and began to fire all the guns that would bear at Fort Griffin. *Sachem* was quickly disabled, with steam pouring onto its deck and scalding the sharpshooters. Following behind, *Arizona* ran aground in the narrow channel.[39]

As the action in the Louisiana channel was winding down, *Clifton* then approached the fort up the Texas channel. Crocker's vessel quickly entered the fort's field of fire and, like *Sachem*, suffered substantial damage to its steering mechanism and steam engine. Deprived of any means of movement, *Clifton* quickly ran aground. Within forty-five minutes after the first Confederate shot had been fired, *Clifton* and *Sachem* were forced to surrender, and the remaining two gunboats retreated out of action. The naval attack had been a complete failure.[40]

Alternative Decisions/Scenario

If the original plan to have the army lead the attack on the fort had been carried out, Fort Griffin likely would have been captured. Although the attack on land might have resulted in significant Union casualties, the fort's incomplete rear wall meant that it could not have survived a sustained siege. In addition, all of Fort Griffin's guns faced the channels at the entrance to the pass. If attempted and properly conducted, a flanking movement on the left would have faced little opposition. If the fort had been captured, it is plausible, even likely, that Franklin's reinforced army of fifteen thousand men would have captured Houston and Galveston within a few weeks. With Texas largely under Union control, Union military planners might then have turned their attention to more strategic targets like Mobile.

Dowling Takes a Vote on Whether to Stay and Fight

Situation

Lieut. Richard "Dick" Dowling was temporarily in charge of the Confederate garrison at Fort Griffin on September 8, 1863. A twenty-six-year-old saloonkeeper in Houston, Dowling was in command of Company F of Cook's First Texas Heavy Artillery, also known as the Davis Guard. The garrison at Fort Griffin included three officers and thirty-eight artillerymen, most of whom were Irish dockworkers and regular customers of Dowling's saloon.[41]

Dowling's orders were to resist enemy attempts to enter Sabine Pass, but he was directed to spike and disable his six guns if faced with an overwhelming force. What qualified as an overwhelming enemy force was left to Dowling's discretion. As the Union's Sabine Pass armada of twenty-six vessels began assembling on September 7, it became apparent that the Confederates were

Lieut. (later Maj.) Richard W. "Dick" Dowling, CSA. AG2008.0005. Lawrence T. Jones III Texas Photography Collection. DeGolyer Library, Southern Methodist University, Dallas.

heavily outnumbered both in terms of personnel (estimated at six thousand versus forty-one) and guns (twenty-six on the gunboats versus six in the fort).[42]

Options

Dowling had three options: ordering his men to disable the guns and retreat, ordering them to stay and fight, or allowing them to vote on whether to stay and fight.

Option 1

Dowling could direct his troops to disable the guns and retreat. Some accounts suggest that Dowling received a written communication from Capt. Frederick Odlum recommending a retreat. Withdrawing would be entirely consistent with the lieutenant's prior orders and was undoubtedly the safest thing to do. Of the six guns in his fort, two were howitzers and of limited utility against ships. Dowling's two heavy guns, the 32-pounders, had been dug out of the ground at Fort Sabine and repaired. Even the engineers who repaired them were uncertain how they might hold up to being repeatedly fired in combat.[43]

Despite the challenges, Dowling was reluctant to retire without a fight. He knew that it would destroy the morale and honor of his men to simply abandon their guns and run away. The lieutenant and his company had worked very hard to get the fort in shape for a major battle. With the help of the engineers, they had determined exactly where each gun would land a projectile at given elevations. The men had then driven stakes into the channel to mark those positions and practiced for hours trying to hit them. Thus the unit was experienced and ready. Dowling did not know when, if ever, Federals would come so cleanly into his prepared field of fire. He had an excellent position. But the enemy had many guns and many men. It would be a definite risk to engage with them.

Option 2

Dowling could order his men to stay and fight. The young lieutenant was personally inclined to stay, believing that his men could do significant damage to the enemy despite the long odds. Dowling was in command at the fort while the captain was away, and it was certainly his call whether to remain or leave. A professional officer would simply make up his mind and announce his decision to those serving under him. But Dowling was a saloonkeeper, not a professional officer.

Dowling knew that confronting the Federals at Fort Griffin would risk the life of every man in the garrison. Given that his orders allowed an honorable retreat, it was a risk that was entirely avoidable. Dowling knew each of his men very well. He had served them beverages before the war and had served with them throughout the conflict. Many were his close personal friends. He was reluctant to make a life-and-death decision for his soldiers without some effort to obtain their consent.

Option 3

Dowling could have his men vote on whether to stay and fight. This option might lead to division in the ranks or produce a result that was contrary to his own judgment. Dowling knew these troops well, however, and he believed that they felt the same way about confronting the enemy as he did. He also believed his men would fight better and harder if they collectively decided to do so instead of having some action forced on them. This was not the orthodox way that military officers handled decision-making, but it was something Dowling might be comfortable with in these unique circumstances.

Decision

Dowling made a few brief remarks to his men about their dangerous situation and then put the issue of engaging the Federals to a vote. After little, if any, discussion, they unanimously decided to stay and fight.[44]

Results/Impact

The decision to stay and fight led directly to Confederate victory at the Battle of Sabine Pass and Union failure to capture Texas. As instructed by the engineers who designed Fort Griffin, Dowling and his men waited to discharge until the Union ships got to the stakes that precisely marked their field of fire. They then fired approximately 137 times from their battery during the space of approximately 45 minutes. This rate is remarkable given that one of the six Confederate guns, a howitzer, recoiled off its platform and was out of action after firing only a couple of times.[45]

Because of their decision to stay and fight, as well as the accuracy of their gunnery, Dowling and his Confederates captured the two leading Union gunboats (*Clifton* and *Sachem*) and forced the remainder to retreat. What was left of the expedition made emergency plans to depart for New Orleans, throwing large quantities of supplies overboard to lighten the ships. Inflicting four hundred casualties on the enemy, Dowling's small company suffered not a single injury from the battle.[46]

"The Disabling and Capture of the Federal Gunboats *Sachem* and *Clifton* in the Attack on Sabine Pass, Texas, September 8, 1863." Line engraving published in *The Soldier in Our Civil War*, volume 2 (1885). NH 59143. US Naval History and Heritage Command.

Dowling's gamble to let the men vote seems to have produced its intended motivational impact. In his short official report written the day after the battle, Dowling did not mention that he had taken a vote. He merely recorded that all his men had behaved like heroes, and not a one had flinched from his post. The lieutenant did note that their collective motto was "Victory or death!" Given the odds the company faced, it is no accident that these words were the concluding line from William Barret Travis's famous letter from the Alamo.[47]

General Weitzel Decides Not to Land His Troops

Situation

The original battle plan agreed on by Captain Crocker and Maj. Gen. William B. Franklin involved a three-pronged assault on Fort Griffin. The first attack would occur when *Sachem* and *Arizona* steamed up the Louisiana channel, drawing the Confederate artillery fire at those gunboats. The second leg of the plan centered on *Clifton*. While the Confederates' guns were firing at the Louisiana channel, Crocker's vessel would use that distraction to dash up the Texas channel directly toward the fort.[48]

In addition to the navy's attacks, a third part of the plan involved a small land assault. This offensive was added to the plan on the day of the battle to make up for the fact that the naval attack was not the surprise at dawn the original strategy contemplated. Brig. Gen. Godfrey Weitzel was ordered to

Brig. Gen. Godfrey Weitzel, USA. LC-DIG-cwpbh-03245. Library of Congress.

load five hundred men onto the transport *General Banks*. He was to land his troops near the site of the old fort, then move north to attack Fort Griffin as soon as *Clifton* began traveling up the Texas channel. With movements from three different directions, this modified plan would hopefully divide and confuse the fort's gunners. [49]

The first part of the scheme misfired quickly, with *Sachem* disabled and *Arizona* aground in the Louisiana channel. The second part of the plan also failed miserably. Shortly after *Clifton* started up the Texas channel, that vessel suffered severe damage to its steam engine and ran aground. Even after that event, the crew on *Clifton* fired on the Confederate fort from their disabled ship for thirty minutes, hoping that the army's promised attack would win the day and save them.[50]

Options

With the gunboats under attack and quickly disabled, Weitzel had two options: land his troops and attack Fort Griffin, or call off the attack and withdraw from action.

Option 1

As he had agreed with Captain Crocker, Weitzel could continue to land his troops and assault Fort Griffin. Technically, Weitzel had agreed to land as soon as the *Clifton* began moving up the channel. But after the failure in the Louisiana channel, he held off on attempting any landing and waited to see what transpired with *Clifton*.

"The Attack on Sabine Pass, September 8, 1863—Sketched by an Eye-Witness." *Harper's Weekly*, October 11, 1863.

As *Clifton* moved rapidly into danger, Weitzel knew that the entire fate of the expedition now lay in his hands. If he landed his troops, his men might save the day for the Union and avoid the capture of two gunboats and their crews. If his assault was successful, the army could now take full credit for capturing Sabine Pass and proceed with the grand plan to capture Houston and Galveston. Weitzel could emerge as the Union hero on a day that so far had not produced any real success stories.

The problem with landing his men and attacking was that Weitzel had waited too long to do so. With the gunboats largely out of action, the Confederates now had time to reposition their guns and decimate his men with canister. It was apparent to Weitzel that the artillerymen in Fort Griffin knew how to effectively fire their guns. The general had no idea how much ammunition the enemy had remaining or what guns might be lurking around the corner of the stronghold. Making landfall in small boats and then marching his men through the mud and up to the fort might be leading them into a massacre. Weitzel had led troops in a similar charge at Port Hudson and had suffered horrendous casualties. He was not eager to repeat that experience.[51]

Option 2

Weitzel could call off the attack and withdraw from action. The general knew that failing to land would effectively kill the Texas expedition's chances. The Confederates would now possess two new gunboats, and the navy would report that the army had failed to live up to its side of the agreed plan of attack. Weitzel might even face personal charges for disobeying orders to land.

Decision

Weitzel called off the attack and withdrew from action. He later attempted to justify his decision by falsely claiming that *Clifton* had grounded at just the spot where he intended to land and thus prevented him from doing so. He also claimed, more convincingly, that the relatively rapid disabling of the Union gunboats made the now-unsupported land portion of the attack too risky to execute. Major General Franklin agreed with this latter excuse, later reporting that Weitzel's part of the plan simply could not be carried out under the circumstances.[52]

Results/Impact

Weitzel's failure to land meant that the Battle of Sabine Pass would end as a stunning Confederate victory. The Sabine Pass expedition that might have led to the capture of Galveston and Houston was now a failure, and what

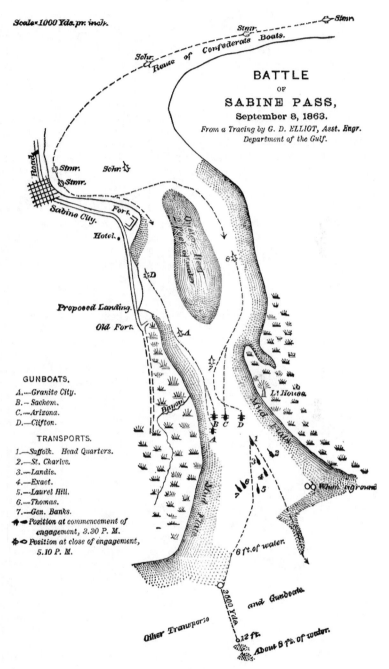

Scale = 1000 Yds. pr. inch.

Route of Confederate Boats.

Stmr.

Sthr.

Stmr.

Stmr.

BATTLE
OF
SABINE PASS,
September 8, 1863.

*From a Tracing by G. D. ELLIOT, Asst. Engr.
Department of the Gulf.*

Road

Stmr.

Stmr.

Schr.

Sabine City.

Fort.

Hotel.

D

Proposed Landing.

Old Fort.

A

Bayou.

GUNBOATS.

A.—Granite City.
B.—Sachem.
C.—Arizona.
D.—Clifton.

TRANSPORTS.

1.—Suffolk. Head Quarters.
2.—St. Charles.
3.—Landis.
4.—Exact.
5.—Laurel Hill.
6.—Thomas.
7.—Gen. Banks.

⚓→ Position at commencement of
    engagement, 3.30 P. M.
⚓→ Position at close of engagement,
    5.10 P. M.

B C D

A

L! House.

Mud Flats.

When aground

6 ft. of water.

and Gunboats.

Other Transports.

2000 Yds.

12 ft.

About 8 ft. of water.

Battle of Sabine Pass map showing ship movements and Weitzel's originally proposed landing site. From a tracing by Asst. Eng. G. D. Elliot. Volume 26 (part 1) of *the Official Records
of the Union and Confederate Armies in the War of the Rebellion.*

was left of its troops limped back to New Orleans. Although General Banks later conceded that the army's landing attempt was feeble at best, neither Weitzel nor Franklin was ever charged with violating orders. Instead, the army would blame the expedition's failure on the inadequacy of the navy's gunboats. Predictably, the navy would blame the disaster of the operation on the army's failure to land and assault the fort as agreed. Ironically, both of these criticisms were largely valid. [53]

Banks had failed to plant the flag in Texas and would have to devise additional operations to accomplish what had at first seemed a relatively simple task. Union military planners never again tested the potential route to Houston and Galveston through Sabine Pass. Banks would have to find a new and more successful avenue if he wanted to threaten the Island City in the future. Yet he was running out of roads. It was time to either get creative or give up.

CHAPTER 5

FROM SABINE PASS TO JUNETEENTH

The failure of the Sabine Pass expedition meant that Major General Banks had a lot of explaining to do. He had to explain to his superiors in Washington, including President Lincoln, why he had made a demonstration on the Louisiana border to convince the French in Mexico of the government's determination to keep Texas in the Union. He then had to explain how a large and well-publicized expedition to plant the flag in Texas had not even managed to land in the state. It was a tall order. Banks wrote Lincoln an extensive letter setting forth the reasoning behind his strategy, trying to convince him that its strategic underpinnings had been sound. Banks continued to maintain that, had it been properly implemented by his subordinates, the plan could and should have resulted in the capture of the key cities of Texas. Knowing that Lincoln probably had little idea where Sabine Pass was, Banks even attached a helpful map showing the pass and the way it might have provided a backdoor route of advance toward Houston and Galveston.[1]

As it turned out, after the Sabine Pass disaster in September 1863, Galveston and Houston remained in Confederate hands for the remainder of the war. Galveston itself would not be occupied by a significant body of Federal troops until June 19, 1865, the original Juneteenth, when Maj. Gen. Gordon Granger arrived and made it the headquarters of the new District of Texas. During this twenty-one-month period between Sabine Pass and Juneteenth, Galveston was threatened by two separate Federal movements, but only from afar. One critical decision kept these threats from achieving meaningful success.

Banks Launches Two Expeditions to Conquer Texas

Situation

Despite his excuses after the Sabine Pass debacle, Banks knew that the clock was still ticking. Lincoln and Halleck had instructed him in no uncertain terms to quickly plant the flag in Texas. This he had so far failed to do. Banks had no alternative but to carry out another assault against Texas. But how and where?

The general had learned from personal experience that sea attacks at Galveston and Sabine Pass would be fiercely contested. Direct operations against those targets were off the table. That left a variety of other potential targets and campaigns. None of them, however, were particularly attractive or offered much strategic benefit. Halleck continued urging Banks to assault east Texas by moving up the Red River and then marching west into the state. But Banks knew the river's water levels were dangerously low and would not support the gunboats vital to any such operation. In addition, it would simply take too long to move a large force up the Red River and cross to any meaningful place in Texas. Ruling out what he thought were the worst options, Banks believed that he was left with only a few to seriously consider.[2]

Options

Banks could land an expedition near the Rio Grande and march up the Texas coast. Alternatively, he could move a force overland from south Louisiana and enter Texas, or he could try a combination of both these plans.

<u>Option 1</u>

Banks's men could disembark near the Rio Grande and march up the Texas coast. This was the cleanest and most obvious way to raise the flag in Texas when Washington was relentlessly pressuring Banks to do so. On some beach near the entrance to the Rio Grande, it seemed very possible that he could land an expedition with little to no opposition. Once onshore, the general could send Washington official confirmation that the flag was now firmly planted in Texas. With that ceremony accomplished, and the pressure somewhat relieved, Banks could develop his landing spot into a beachhead through which he could funnel a substantial invasion force. It would not be easy, but that force could then move up the coast overland and, with support from naval gunboats, overcome the various Confederate land fortifications.

At the end of this long road (roughly four hundred miles) lay Galveston, the elusive prize that Banks still believed was distantly within his reach. The general had originally chosen the Sabine Pass expedition landing site because he thought it might provide a backdoor route to seize Houston and cut off Galveston from the railroad network in the interior. Studying his maps, Banks saw that a Rio Grande operation represented a similar, albeit much longer, route coming up the Texas coast from the opposite direction. After an extended march, a Rio Grande expedition might eventually reach the western shore of Galveston Bay, where Banks could conceivably avoid the defenses of Galveston Island entirely and simply sever the railroad line to Houston.

The problem with this option was the same one that had previously made Banks reject the Rio Grande operation in favor of his Sabine Pass expedition. Taking any sizable force up the Texas coast from the south involved long marches over inhospitable areas with little food, water, or wood. Even if the logistics and supply issues could be resolved, the Texas coast had a large number of bays and rivers that would need to be crossed. Banks knew that the Confederates had fortifications at some of these positions. He also knew that as he got closer to Galveston, Magruder's Confederates would eventually advance and put up heavy resistance to every crossing. This would make movement extremely difficult and costly—a campaign up the Texas coast might take months, even years. Banks questioned whether he had the necessary resources and support from his superiors for such a sustained campaign to succeed. The journey was potentially a dangerous proposition.

Option 2

Banks could move a force overland from south Louisiana and enter Texas. He had ruled out advancing up the Red River to the north because it would take too long and require use of a river with too little water. He had also ruled out repeating his unsuccessful attempt to land at Sabine Pass on the coast. However, there was still one operation through the Bayou Country of Louisiana that might accomplish his original Sabine Pass objective. Banks began exploring a plan to take a sizable army up Bayou Teche to the area around Vermilionville (modern-day Lafayette) and then march it westward across the prairie into Texas. The potential point of entry would be in the vicinity of Niblett's Bluff, a settlement on the Louisiana side of the Sabine River about ten miles northeast of Orange, Texas.[3]

Although it would not plant the flag in Texas very fast, Banks believed that this Texas Overland Campaign option, as it came to be called, stood a good chance of success. On paper, he had sufficient resources for the task. He had put together an army of almost thirty thousand men, the largest ever assembled in the Trans-Mississippi during the war. It had not only a large infantry force, but also a strong component of cavalry. Coming west from Louisiana meant that, in theory, this force could pass well north of the Confederate fort at Sabine Pass. It would instead proceed directly to the railroad line extending west from Orange to Houston. In effect, these troops would accomplish exactly what Banks had originally intended at Sabine Pass without the necessity of transporting troops by sea and landing under fire at the pass.[4]

Although this option looked good on paper, it faced a number of practical challenges. First, the troops that would be employed in this operation were not as cohesive as Banks might have desired. The largest unit, the Thirteenth Army Corps, consisted of tough westerners who were veterans of the Vicksburg Campaign. The remaining troops were from the Nineteenth Corps, which included primarily men from Massachusetts, New York, and Pennsylvania. Maj. Gen. William B. Franklin had been present at the Sabine Pass debacle. He would be in overall command of the unit and was well aware that the men of these two corps did not know, like, or even trust one another. It would be a challenge for any general to mold these troops into an effective fighting force, and Franklin had shown little capability to achieve this result.[5]

The second obstacle that Banks had to consider was the Confederate army. Landing a force near the Rio Grande would have the element of surprise and would be unlikely to involve any serious conflict with the enemy. The same could not be said about an overland movement from Louisiana to Texas. Maj. Gen. Richard Taylor, son of former president Zachary Taylor, was in charge of the Confederate army in the District of Western Louisiana. It was certainly a much smaller force than Franklin would command. But the men were well led, and they knew the country that they would be defending exceptionally well. Banks anticipated that once it was apparent that an operation was headed toward Texas from Louisiana, General Magruder would hurry troops over from Texas to supplement Taylor's army. Taylor's troops already included a Texas contingent commanded by Gen. Thomas "Tom" Green, who had been a significant participant in the Confederate victory at Galveston. The bottom line was that Banks did not entirely trust his own force and had reason to be concerned about the capabilities of the Confederates they would encounter.[6]

Another significant factor arguing against an overland campaign from Louisiana to Texas was geography. Generals Grant and Sherman had shown that it was possible to successfully move large armies through Confederate territory, subsisting on rations gathered from the enemy's farms and towns. The movement that Banks was considering, however, was much more problematic. Marching west from Louisiana to a target like Houston involved a distance of over two hundred miles. The area between the Teche and the Texas border was sparsely settled prairie where "living off the land" would be difficult. Supporting a large army and associated cavalry without the benefit of boats, railroads, and roads would be a daunting proposition.[7]

Option 3

Banks could attempt a combination of both plans. While Franklin started a movement up the Teche and advanced westward to threaten the Texas border, a separate force could plant the flag at the Rio Grande and begin the movement up the Texas coast. Banks believed that Magruder lacked sufficient forces to deal with two simultaneous threats coming from opposite directions. With any luck, he would divide his forces and respond more strongly to one of the two dangers. Banks would then use whichever route seemed less contested to approach Houston and Galveston.[8]

On paper, this option looked extremely interesting. It was usually a good strategy to keep an enemy guessing about your plan of attack. Coming at Galveston by land from opposite directions would certainly mean that Magruder could not respond to either threat with his full force. Another advantage of this strategy was that it did not involve movements by ships against strong shore fortifications, a factor that had led to ignominious defeat at Sabine Pass. The fact that the plan contemplated land movements also meant that Magruder could not employ cottonclad gunboats, vessels that had been the key to several prior Union disasters. It would force the unconventional Magruder to mount a more conventional defense.

If the dual-expedition plan was properly implemented, Banks believed that it could potentially result in the complete capture of Texas, with victory in Louisiana not far behind. Such results would remove the stain of the Sabine Pass disaster forever and enable Banks to claim credit as the architect of one of the boldest and most successful campaigns of the war. The general still had political aspirations and suspected that headlines trumpeting his seizure of Texas might help his political career.[9]

If the dual-expedition strategy was appealing in concept, carrying the plan out would be extremely challenging. It was almost six hundred miles from the Rio Grande, where the potential western expedition would start, to Lafayette, Louisiana, where the potential eastern expedition would start. In between were Taylor's and Magruder's Confederate armies and their improvised cottonclad navy. Coordinating two expeditions at locations so far apart would be impossible. Banks could be present at only one of the two sites. It would also be extremely difficult to provide simultaneous support and supplies to two such widely separated forces.

Banks had not asked for or received General Halleck's blessing for the dual-expedition strategy. As Banks knew, Halleck still favored a larger movement up the Red River. He had previously warned Banks against sending a force to the Rio Grande, noting the obvious difficulties of managing an army at such a distance with the enemy in the middle. Halleck had a point. Two expeditions meant twice the risk. Although Banks could imagine the glory that might attend two successful expeditions, he also knew that two high profile disasters would probably finish both his military and political careers.

Decision

Banks decided to launch two expeditions. He ordered General Franklin to head up the Louisiana operation, which began slowly advancing up the Teche in early October. The Rio Grande expedition, which departed about three weeks later, was placed under the command of Maj. Gen. Napoleon Jackson Tecumseh Dana. Banks would make brief appearances on both expeditions but did not direct any troops in combat operations.

Results/Impact

Banks's decision to launch two operations was the last critical decision that helped Galveston remain in Confederate hands until the very end of the war. Commencing two weak campaigns instead of one strong campaign was a major error. By dividing his forces and attempting two operations from opposite directions, Banks deprived both missions of the direction and resources that could have resulted in their success. Failing to fully support one force and operation ensured that neither force or operation had the strength to fight its way into range of capturing Galveston or Houston. Although General Banks's choice to launch both expeditions eventually established a Federal presence in south Texas, thus granting President Lincoln's wish for a symbolic Union presence in the state, both operations stalled for lack of guidance and means. As a result, neither expedition got close enough to Galveston to seriously threaten it. The Louisiana expedition never left Louisiana, and the Rio Grande expedition took too long and never got within a hundred miles of the city before it was recalled.

By October 9, 1863, the Louisiana expedition under Franklin's direction reached Vermilionville, which was near the area where this force was to turn and head west toward Texas. Knowing that this expedition was now reaching a critical point, Banks came up from New Orleans to confer with General Franklin and witness the occupation of this important town. Banks was disappointed to learn that the situation at Vermilionville was not conducive to any immediate operations against Texas. Union scouts reported a strong Confederate presence in the area. Even worse, preliminary reconnaissance of the route leading west to Texas heightened concerns about the absence of water, food, and necessary provisions. Banks was forced to write President Lincoln and advise him that, for the time being, the overland route to Texas seemed to face "insuperable difficulties."[10]

After leaving Franklin at Vermilionville with a confusing set of instructions that did not direct him to do much of anything, Banks returned to New Orleans. On October 26, 1863, the general set sail for the Rio Grande with an expedition of six thousand men. The plan for this western expedition was to land at Brazos Santiago, a village on Brazos Island near the entrance to the Rio Grande. After a very rough passage, Banks stepped ashore at Brazos Island on November 1, 1863. His landing was unopposed. The general wasted no time in informing Lincoln and his other superiors that his latest plan had been a complete success. Belatedly, the Union flag had been planted on Texas soil.[11]

While General Banks was planting the flag on a Texas beach and calling on Washington for reinforcements, General Franklin found his Louisiana expedition largely stalled. He had settled his command near Opelousas and repeatedly requested definite instructions from Banks. Was he to move his command toward Texas or not? Because Banks was preparing to head to Texas, Franklin received no answer. With no clear objective, on October 26 Franklin started to move his army back south. Some elements were sent ahead toward the coast, where they were surprised to learn they were to board transports to Texas to join the Rio Grande expedition.[12]

Running short on supplies, Franklin's retreating army was scattered along a narrow road near Grand Coteau. On November 3, 1863, Taylor's Confederates launched a surprise assault against the rear portion of the column. Several regiments of Union troops broke and ran. The Battle of Bayou Bourbeau,

"Landing of General Banks's Expedition on Brazos Santiago," as sketched by a staff officer. *Harper's Weekly*, November 28, 1863.

as the action later became known, resulted in a major victory for the Confederates. What was left of Franklin's Union army continued to withdraw. This effectively ended the so-called Texas Overland Expedition of 1863, which never came close to reaching Texas.[13]

If Banks had stayed with Franklin and the Louisiana expedition, and placed his full resources behind that campaign, it is possible, even likely, that the Federals could have forced their way west and eventually captured Galveston and Houston. Franklin had sought Banks's authorization to retreat to New Iberia, then proceed west toward Texas from that more easily supplied position. This proposal received no response because Banks had already left for the Rio Grande. By draining essential troops and resources away from Franklin, and then basically abandoning him in enemy country with no direction or instructions, Banks ensured that Franklin's operation would be a complete fiasco. As a result, the Louisiana expedition never got close enough to threaten Galveston.[14]

Over in south Texas, the Rio Grande expedition started off with much more promise. After wading ashore and raising the flag, Banks returned to New Orleans at the beginning of December. General Dana then continued pressing his troops slowly but methodically up the coast. By January 1, 1864, the Union force had captured Corpus Christi, Indianola, and Port Lavaca. To reach Galveston and Houston, the expedition would still need to continue slogging its way up the Matagorda Peninsula and then cross several rivers. Scouts reported a Confederate fort at each of those river crossings. The enemy seemed to have a particularly strong line of defense near Caney Creek. When reconnaissance confirmed that these fortifications were unexpectedly substantial, Banks worried that he lacked sufficient troops to accomplish the task. As he now belatedly realized, many of these needed men were still languishing with Franklin in Louisiana.[15]

With insufficient men and supplies to continue an aggressive campaign up the Texas coast, and with no support from Washington for further movement, the expedition from the Rio Grande stalled. By January 1864, Banks became tired of defending the potential merits of his Rio Grande operation. As a skilled politician, he knew that it was time to switch tactics. Banks told his superiors that he now favored Halleck's idea of a campaign up the Red River in Louisiana. To show his commitment, Banks began shipping troops back from Texas to Louisiana. What was left of the Rio Grande expedition now became nothing more than a token force keeping Magruder's attention away from Louisiana, where preparations were underway for the Red River expedition. By March 1864, Ulysses S. Grant had become general-in-chief and ordered the abandonment of the entire Texas coast except for the Brownsville area. Like its counterpart in Louisiana, the Rio Grande campaign in Texas was now officially a failure.[16]

Alternate Decision/Scenario

Although neither of the two expeditions that Banks launched accomplished anything substantial, either one of them might have succeeded if given all the general's resources. Franklin initially had a large enough army on the Teche in Louisiana to be a serious threat if it reached Texas. Although Banks had quite rightly worried about supplying a force moving through Louisiana toward Houston, the difficulties might have been overcome with rationing, staging of supplies, and some effort. Late in the war, George Armstrong Custer successfully led a column of cavalry west from Alexandria, Louisiana, to the Houston area. If Banks had placed all his resources behind Franklin's Louisiana expedition, Galveston and Houston might possibly have fallen to the Union in late 1863 or 1864.[17]

Similarly, if Banks had immediately sent Franklin and his troops to south Texas and mounted a fully supported expedition up from the Rio Grande, the Federals possibly, even likely, would have moved faster up the coast, overcome Magruder's defenses, and captured Galveston. Ironically, Banks's Rio Grande operation, which no one in Washington seemed to appreciate or support, might have come the closest to success of any Union campaign in the Lone Star State. In the later stages of the Texas coastal campaign, Banks began to see a tantalizing light at the end of the tunnel. One historian of this campaign has observed that if Banks had only been granted sufficient time and reinforcements, his army could have brushed aside the Confederate troops on the Caney River, where he would then have found "a clear road to Galveston."[18] By marching two long and complicated roads to Galveston, Banks stopped well short of the destination.

CHAPTER 6

AFTERWARD AND CONCLUSIONS

On the morning of June 5, 1865, Capt. Benjamin Sands of the US Navy came ashore in Galveston and witnessed the raising of his country's flag above the 1861 customhouse. He regarded this as "pleasant duty" because it represented the "closing act of the great rebellion." Because Galveston had not been as devastated by the war as cities in other Confederate states, it quickly resumed its status as the largest Texas city and one of the most rapidly growing port cities in America. Providing expanded railroad service to that port, Houston also successfully bounced back after the war. When the Island City was almost destroyed by the Great Storm of 1900, Houston stepped in to fill the void, in the process beginning to shape its destiny as one of the largest and most successful American cities.[1]

Galveston ended up being the last major Confederate port because of a variety of decisions. As detailed in this work, twenty-one of those decisions (hereinafter referred to as the "Galveston decisions") were critical decisions. Made over four years, these were of sufficient magnitude to shape subsequent events in a way that kept Galveston in Confederate hands until the end of the war. Having identified those choices and their consequences, it may be useful to now analyze and characterize them on a broader scale.

One of the first things that will strike every reader of this book is how many of the Galveston decisions were actually made outside the city—fourteen of the twenty-one critical decisions fit this description. Jefferson Davis's choice to send Magruder to Texas, for example, was made in Richmond, Virginia. Magruder's plans for the Battle of Galveston were drawn up in

Houston or en route to that city. Farragut's decisions not to allow Renshaw to withdraw and not to go to Galveston after its loss were both made at New Orleans. President Lincoln mandated the Texas campaign resulting in the Battle of Sabine Pass while he was in Washington, DC. All of Banks's decisions relating to the Texas operations were made in Louisiana.

The critical decisions outlined in this book tended to be made outside Galveston because they were generally strategic rather than tactical in nature. Tactical decisions, meaning those directing forces during the course of a battle, were relatively few. That does not mean that these choices were unimportant. On the contrary, if Maj. Leon Smith had not continued his naval attack, the Battle of Galveston would have ended immediately as a Union victory. On the Union side, if Brigadier General Weitzel had landed his troops at the Battle of Sabine Pass, that battle might well have ended up as a Union victory and been the beginning of a successful campaign against Galveston.

An interesting feature of the Galveston decisions is the wide differences in rank of the officers who made them. Two of the most important decisions—Jefferson Davis sending Magruder to Texas and Abraham Lincoln mandating a Texas campaign—were made at the commander-in-chief level. Equally if not more important, however, was the decision of twenty-six-year-old Confederate lieutenant Dick Dowling, who ignored orders that would have allowed him to evacuate his fort at Sabine Pass and instead persuaded his small company of artillerymen to stay and fight. It is difficult to think of another consequential battle of the war that was largely decided by the actions of such a youthful and low-ranking officer.

As Dowling's example points out, it is certainly not uncommon for the identity of a commander to determine the outcome of a battle. That was particularly the case in the Texas engagements. Several of the Galveston decisions revolved around selection of personnel. The Battle of Galveston certainly would not have been fought the way it was, and might not have been fought at all, if Jefferson Davis had not sent Magruder to command in Texas. Likewise, Magruder's choice of Leon Smith to head up the naval part of his plan of attack was a key factor—probably *the* key factor—in its success.

An interesting feature of the Galveston decisions that distinguishes them from those made in many other Civil War battles is their focus on ship movements or encounters between ships and shore artillery positions. All of the battles affecting Galveston involved naval elements, and one, the capture of *Hatteras* by *Alabama*, was fought purely at sea out of sight of land. Many Confederate states had actions involving naval conflicts on their coasts or rivers. Texas was unique, however, in that essentially all its major battles occurred either on the water or only a short distance from the shore.

The fact that many of the critical decisions identified in this book involve naval operations makes them particularly interesting to analyze. Banks and Magruder were both army generals called on to plan operations involving important contributions from marine forces not under their immediate command. That these operations largely succeeded for Magruder and failed for Banks does not appear to be due to any superior nautical skill or insight that Magruder possessed. Instead, Union naval failures owed in large part to the particular deficiencies of the ships employed (e.g., the sinking of *Hatteras* and the capture of *Morning Light*), or the way in which the navy volunteered to directly engage a Confederate fort (Battle of Sabine Pass).

This book began with a section defining what a critical decision is and what it is not. One point made in that discussion is that a decision may turn out to be critically important for reasons that are not apparent when it is made. In fact, some choices have significant consequences simply as a result of chance. This is certainly true of the Galveston decisions. On the night of January 1, 1863, Commodore Renshaw happened to run aground in Galveston Bay at just the wrong moment, and then was killed when the explosive charge he rigged to destroy his ship exploded prematurely. Luck can also make a decision appear smarter than it actually was. Raphael Semmes decided to take *Alabama* to Galveston, where he managed to lure out and sink the Union steamer *Hatteras*. However, he headed for Galveston based on a completely erroneous assumption about the situation there, including his misidentification of the side in possession of the city. Semmes was also lucky that only *Hatteras*, a clearly inferior ship, was sent out to encounter *Alabama*.

What lessons can be learned from the critical decisions that determined which side ultimately controlled Galveston? First, since every choice may be important and have unforeseen consequences, it is important to make decisions deliberately and carefully. Jefferson Davis did not and could not know that sending Magruder to Texas would be the first link in a chain of events making Texas the most successfully defended Confederate state. Similarly, Magruder and his engineers could not and did not know that relocating and rebuilding the fort at Sabine Pass would result in one of the greatest David over Goliath victories in military history. These decisions were made not because of brilliant insight, but simply because they were appropriate based on the best available information.

A second lesson from the Galveston decisions relates to strategy. Because plans of attack famously do not survive first contact with an enemy, there is a tendency to avoid making them too complicated. But a simple scheme (sending four gunboats to directly attack the Sabine Pass fort) does not always succeed. Also, a complex and highly unorthodox plan (Magruder's at the Battle of Galveston) may occasionally work because it offers more ways to defeat an unprepared opponent. This is not to say that a complicated plan of attack always or even usually stands a greater chance of success. In late 1863, Banks's two-pronged assault against Galveston from Louisiana and the Rio Grande turned out to involve one prong too many and materially weakened his chance of victory.

The last lesson from the Galveston decisions is that sometimes the best decision is made with emotion rather than calculation. On the afternoon of September 8, 1863, Dick Dowling and his forty men were facing an armada at the entrance to Sabine Pass. The saloonkeeper was probably unaware of military theory and had almost certainly never studied military tactics. What Dowling did know was the nature and character of the men around him. He knew what they were capable of and how they would respond to a stressful and dangerous situation. He asked them to vote to stay and fight because he believed that was the right thing to do. Dowling "trusted his gut," in the language of today. Trusting the people around him, the drills they had conducted, and the engineers who had put them in a position to succeed became perhaps the most critical of all the critical decisions keeping Galveston in Confederate hands. Recognizing the bravery of Dowling and his troops at the Battle of Sabine Pass, the people of Galveston and Houston took up a collection to produce silver medals for every man in the fort that day. Because they were accompanied by a resolution of thanks from the Confederate Congress, these medals are sometimes considered the only medals officially authorized for bravery in the Confederacy.[2]

The fact that Galveston remained under Confederate control was of importance to a wider audience than the few thousand Texas residents who called the island their home. Prominent historians have argued persuasively that the Union's Red River Campaign in Louisiana and the resulting delay in attacking Mobile might have prolonged the Civil War and resulted in thousands of unnecessary casualties on both sides.[3] If this argument is correct, then it is important to understand the cause behind these mistakes. Union war planners' continued belief in the necessity of launching and continuing to support the disastrous Texas Campaigns created this devastating misallocation of military resources.

Because the Union never effectively controlled Galveston and the railroad network circling Houston, military planners in Washington and their subordinates in New Orleans never believed they had a firm grasp on Texas. Thus they remained all too focused on this increasingly problematic theater of operations. Union commanders could have turned their attention to more productive operations in the East (such as the capture of Mobile). Instead, they commenced a series of ever more costly and ineffective efforts like the Red River expedition that were designed to plant the flag in Texas and take control of the Lone Star State. These operations produced only a series of colossal failures. The critical decisions discussed herein ensured that the last United States flag raised over a major Confederate port would not fly until Captain Sands, a naval officer, brought it ashore at Galveston on June 5, 1865.

APPENDIX I

A BATTLEFIELD GUIDE
TO THE TEXAS CAMPAIGNS

1. Palmito Ranch and Banks Landing Site

There are no national Civil War battlefield parks in Texas as there are in other states. The only federally commemorated site is the Palmito Ranch National Historic Landmark in deep south Texas near the border with Mexico. You may view the historic marker for the battle at 43296 Palmito Hill Road, Brownsville, TX 78521. The Battle of Palmito Ranch was the final land battle of the American Civil War. It was fought May 12–13, 1865, along the banks of the Rio Grande, thirteen miles east of Brownsville and ten miles from the Union-held seaport of Los Brazos de Santiago at Texas's southern tip. This Confederate victory took place more than a month after Gen. Robert E. Lee's surrender of the Army of Northern Virginia to Union forces, and thirteen days before the Army of the Trans-Mississippi surrendered in Galveston on May 26. Historical markers are situated nearby, and a US Fish and Wildlife Service viewing platform with interpretive signage is located at the intersection of Palmito Hill Road and Boca Chica Highway (HWY 4).

A number of the critical decisions discussed in this book involve Union plans to protect and strengthen the border between Texas and Mexico. Palmito Ranch is very close to the border, and it reflects the tensions affecting the region on both sides of the border throughout the war. The Palmito Ranch battle occurred too late to play any part in the Civil War's outcome.

However, this engagement is unique for involving a Confederate force including a large contingent of Hispanic soldiers, and a Federal force including a large contingent of Black soldiers. The site of the battle is today largely undeveloped rural area.

Not far from Palmito Ranch at Brazos Santiago is the site where Maj. Gen. Nathaniel Banks landed to finally plant the Union flag in Texas. That event, central to several critical decisions in this book, is commemorated by a Texas historical marker labeled "Brazos Santiago, C.S.A." This memorial is located at Isla Blanca Park at Wells Point, near the intersection of Channel View Road and State Park Road 100. It is interesting to note that the Banks landing site would today be within easy viewing of the SpaceX launch facility at nearby Boca Chica.

The address for Isla Blanca Park is 33174 State Park Road 100, South Padre Island, TX 78597. Banks waded ashore near here at noon on November 2, 1863, and immediately sent a dispatch to Washington confirming his landing.

Report of Maj. Gen. Nathaniel P. Banks, Commanding Department of the Gulf, United States Army

The flag of the Union floated over Texas today at meridian precisely. Our enterprise has been a complete success. Make preparations for movements as directed. Details tomorrow. [N. P. Banks to Brig. Gen. C. P. Stone, Chief of Staff, Off Brazos, TX, November 2, 1863, *OR* [Part 1], 26:396. Similar dispatch sent to Pres. A. Lincoln dated November 3, 1863]

2. Battle of Galveston

Stop 1—Strand Walking Tour and Site of Magruder's First Shot

Despite the absence of national military parks, there are several interesting sites in Texas associated with the battles discussed in this book. The most important battlefield, of course, is at Galveston itself. Galveston is on the island of the same name, about fifty-one miles from Houston. A historical marker describing the Battle of Galveston is located at the Texas Seaport Museum, 2200 Harborside Drive, Galveston, TX 77550. The museum is at Pier 22 adjacent to the 1877 tall ship *Elissa*. In addition to covering *Elissa*'s story and Galveston's maritime history, the museum has a database that allows visitors to

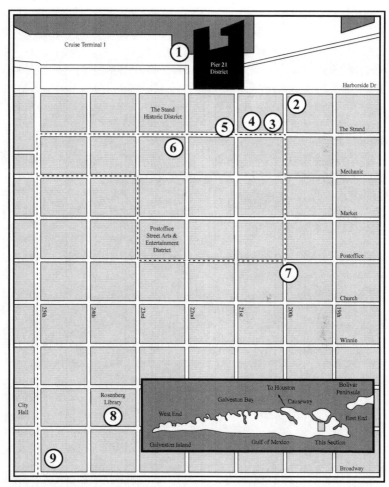

1. Battle of Galveston historical marker at the Texas Seaport Museum
2. Peanut Butter Warehouse and site of the first shot of the Battle of Galveston
3. Battle damage to the column on the Hendley Building
4. Hendley Row Building (1855-1859)
5. Site of Lieut. Sidney Sherman's mortal wounding
6. Site of the Osterman Building and Juneteenth Mural
7. 1861 US Custom House and Official Texas Battlefield Marker
8. Rosenberg Library archives and museum
9. Site of General Magruder's battle headquarters

····· Downtown
      Trolley
      Route

Civil War Galveston Walking Tour Map

search the names of more than 133,000 immigrants who entered the country through Galveston, once known as the Ellis Island of the West. The Seaport Museum stands on land reclaimed from the waters of Galveston Bay after the Civil War. In 1863 the city's shore was across Avenue A, appropriately named Harborside Drive.

One of Major General Magruder's most critical decisions in planning the Battle of Galveston involved a bombardment from the shore against the Union fleet. His line of artillery would extend for about two and one-half miles along the waterfront. The central part of the Confederate line of battle traced the general contours of modern-day Harborside Drive. Readers will not go far wrong in imagining a Confederate battery facing out at the water near the intersection of virtually every numbered street and Harborside for many blocks east and west of Twentieth Street. I recommend beginning a Battle of Galveston walking tour at the Hendley Row Building, 2016 Strand Street, Galveston, TX 77550. As its name suggests, the Hendley Row Building was actually a series of separate structures built in stages between 1855 and 1859 and then covered with a unified facade. This building, the tallest in Galveston at the time of the Civil War, was part of the center of the line of Confederate artillery that Magruder moved into position on the morning of January 1, 1863.

If you walk north on Twentieth Street from the Strand toward Harborside (keeping the Hendley Building on your left), you will see on your right the Peanut Butter Warehouse (100 Twentieth Street). This postwar structure has a good historic marker on its porch displaying a photograph of Kuhn's Wharf and the land portion of the Battle of Galveston. Kuhn's Wharf was located two blocks away at the foot of Eighteenth Street, and the photo on display here was taken from the top of the Hendley Building in 1861. Proceeding back south toward the Strand (Avenue B), you will see a manhole cover in the center of Twentieth Street. This is the approximate location of Wilson's Battery, from which Major General Magruder fired the first shot of the Battle of Galveston. According to an eyewitness, Magruder discharged the gun at this location and then said, "Now, boys, I have done my job as a private, I will go attend to that of General" [Hayes, *Galveston*, 2:55].

The Hendley Building itself (Twentieth and Strand) is closely associated with the battle. An eyewitness drawing of the battle in Galveston's Rosenberg Library (2310 Sealy Avenue) shows Confederate guns firing out the rear second-story windows of this structure. I believe that these guns were probably howitzers. The rear of the Hendley Building shows significant damage to its brick surface, but it is difficult to determine what portion of the damage we see today was caused by the Union bombardment during the Battle of

Approximate location of the first shot at the Battle of
Galveston, January 1, 1863. Author's collection.

Galveston, and what was caused by several devastating storms and natural ca-
tastrophes. On the side of the Hendley Building, however, the top of the seventh column heading north on Twentieth Street from the Strand still shows
significant injury from the battle. Based on the angle of fire, a shell launched
from USS *Owasco* was likely the culprit.

Report of Maj. Gen. John B. Magruder, Commanding District of Texas, New Mexico and Arizona, Confederate States Army

Leading the center assault in person, I approached within two
squares of the wharves, at which point I directed the horses of the
field pieces to be removed from them and placed behind some brick
buildings for shelter from the anticipated discharges of grape and
canister. . . . The guns were placed along a line of about 2 1/2 miles,

Hendley Building column top damaged during the
Battle of Galveston. Author's collection.

principally within the limits of the city. It having been agreed that
the fire of the center gun should furnish signal for a general attack,
I proceeded to carry out this portion of the plan by discharging the
piece myself. The signal was promptly responded to by an almost
simultaneous and very effective discharge along the whole line. The
moon had by that time gone down, but still the light of the stars
enabled us to see the Federal ships. The enemy did not hesitate long
in replying to our attack. He soon opened on us from his fleet with
a tremendous discharge of shell, which was followed with grape and
canister. [J. B. Magruder to S. Cooper, Galveston, TX, February 26,
1863, *OR*, 15:214]

Walking west on Strand in front of the Hendley Building and continuing
to Twenty-First Street, you will reach an intersection near the location of
the Confederate battery commanded by Lieut. Sidney Sherman. Sherman's

father, who had the same name, was the famous commander of the left wing of the Texian Army at the Battle of San Jacinto. The young Sherman, between nineteen and twenty-one years old by various accounts, was mortally wounded early in the Battle of Galveston. His last words were reported as follows: "Tell my father and mother that I fell beside my gun, and that I die happy in behalf of my country" [Cotham, *Battle on the Bay*, 11].

Stop 2—Juneteenth and Nia Cultural Center

Continuing to walk west down the Strand (Avenue B), at Twenty-Second Street visitors will be unable to miss a five-thousand-square-foot mural titled *Absolute Equality* on the side of the Old Galveston Square Building. At this intersection, today a parking lot, stood the Osterman Building. A historical marker on Strand at Twenty-Second describes the events that took place here. On June 19, 1865, a staff officer for Maj. Gen Gordon Granger issued an order proclaiming, "All slaves are free." This order and its date of issuance gave rise to the nation's newest national holiday. The colorful mural includes depictions of Granger signing an order while backed by Black soldiers from the United States Colored Troops.

Behind the Juneteenth mural is the Nia Cultural Center, 2217 Strand Street, Suite 101, Galveston, TX 77550. The Nia Center includes the Juneteenth Legacy Project Headquarters and art gallery. The gallery offers a unique journey through African American history from the 1800s to the present day, featuring sculptures and paintings by local Black artists, plus a reflection area. A number of these art projects involve Juneteenth or other Civil War subjects. A portion of the building housing the Nia Center incorporates the 1857 E. S. Wood Building. Guides in the gallery frequently point out bricks in this old section that preserve the finger marks of enslaved people who helped make them and construct the building.

General Orders No. 3 (the Juneteenth Order), Issued at the Headquarters of Maj. Gen. Gordon Granger, Commanding District of Texas, United States Army

The people of Texas are informed that in accordance with a proclamation from the Executive of the United States, "all slaves are free." This involves an absolute equality of personal rights and rights of property between former masters and slaves, and the connection heretofore existing between them becomes that between employer and hired labor. The freedmen are advised to remain at their present homes and work for wages. They are informed that they will not be allowed to collect at military posts; and they will not be supported in idleness either there or elsewhere. [Order signed by Maj. and A.A.G. F. W. Emery, Galveston, TX, June 19, 1865, *OR*, 48:929]

Stop 3—1861 US Custom House and Postoffice Street

The official Texas battlefield monument for the Battle of Galveston is located at the 1861 United States Custom House and Courthouse, 1918 Postoffice Street, Galveston, TX 77550. This impressive brick building, the first nonmilitary building constructed by the federal government in Texas, made extensive use of iron in its structural elements. It was one of the first places where the Juneteenth Order was printed and posted.

After Union forces captured Galveston in October 1862, their first destination was the customhouse, where Capt. Jonathan M. Wainwright personally raised the United States flag over the building. All of the marines in the shore party were proud of what they considered an important accomplishment.

Account by Pvt. Henry O. Gusley, Marine Guard of USS *Westfield*, of the Raising of the Flag at the US Custom House on October 9, 1862

We found the wharves of the town guarded by the firemen in full uniform, by orders of the Mayor, and on landing they escorted us to the custom-house. The Mayor here received us, and expressed his pleasure at seeing the city once more pass into Union hands. He delivered the keys to Capt. Wainwright who immediately took possession of the building and proceeded to the roof with a proper guard and raised the flag. The battalion presented arms as the colors were flung to the breeze, and the crowd of spectators expressed their delight in various patriotic remarks. Altogether it was quite a gala occasion for the marines and sailors and when we marched back to the boats nearly every one of our muskets was decorated with flowers, which the women and children gave to us. Of the people of Galveston we must say, that a more respectable and well-behaved set we have never seen. [Cotham, *Southern Journey of a Civil War Marine*, 106–7]

I recommend that visitors walk to the rear of the building after viewing its impressive columned facade. During the Battle of Galveston, the main Confederate reserves from the Sibley Brigade were positioned behind this building.

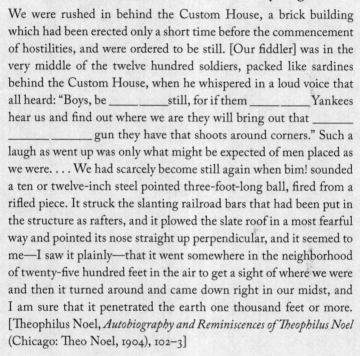

Account of Sgt. Maj. Theophilus Noel, Fourth Texas Mounted Volunteers, First Texas Cavalry Brigade

We were rushed in behind the Custom House, a brick building which had been erected only a short time before the commencement of hostilities, and were ordered to be still. [Our fiddler] was in the very middle of the twelve hundred soldiers, packed like sardines behind the Custom House, when he whispered in a loud voice that all heard: "Boys, be _____ _____still, for if them _____ _____Yankees hear us and find out where we are they will bring out that _____ _____ _____ gun they have that shoots around corners." Such a laugh as went up was only what might be expected of men placed as we were. . . . We had scarcely become still again when bim! sounded a ten or twelve-inch steel pointed three-foot-long ball, fired from a rifled piece. It struck the slanting railroad bars that had been put in the structure as rafters, and it plowed the slate roof in a most fearful way and pointed its nose straight up perpendicular, and it seemed to me—I saw it plainly—that it went somewhere in the neighborhood of twenty-five hundred feet in the air to get a sight of where we were and then it turned around and came down right in our midst, and I am sure that it penetrated the earth one thousand feet or more. [Theophilus Noel, *Autobiography and Reminiscences of Theophilus Noel* (Chicago: Theo Noel, 1904), 102–3]

Also on Postoffice, just a few steps from the customhouse, is the site where Confederate major general Braxton Bragg collapsed and died on September 27, 1876. Galveston's 1894 Grand Opera House is also located in this same block, at 2020 Postoffice. A remarkable coincidence is that the first prominent actress to play the new theater in January 1895 was Marie Wainwright. She was the daughter of Capt. Jonathan Wainwright, who had raised the flag over the nearby US Custom House and was later killed in the Battle of Galveston. While Marie was in Galveston, the widow of a Confederate soldier presented her with a sword said to have belonged to her father. The soldier had apparently picked it up on the deck of the *Harriet Lane*.

Stop 4—Rosenberg Library and Magruder's Headquarters

The Galveston and Texas History Center of the Rosenberg Library, located at 2310 Sealy Avenue, Galveston, Texas 77550, has a number of interesting displays relating to the Battle of Galveston. In addition, the center has several eyewitness depictions and drawings of the battle in its collection. The library's museum exhibits a variety of artifacts, including shell fragments and captured swords. Two blocks away, Major General Magruder's headquarters during the Battle of Galveston was at a home (no longer standing) near the northeast corner of Twenty-Fifth Street and Broadway (Avenue J). He relied on reports from scouts situated on the roof at a nearby building, probably the 1859 Ashton Villa, which is located at 2328 Broadway (Avenue J), Galveston, TX 77550. This historic home, available for tours and events today, was also the site of a visit by former president U. S. Grant in 1880.

The monuments for the Union and Confederate casualties of the Battle of Galveston both stand about fifteen blocks down Broadway in the Trinity Episcopal Cemetery. Trinity is one of seven cemeteries along Broadway (Avenue J) extending from Fortieth Street to Forty-Third Street. Specifically, it is in the southeastern part of the complex, adjacent to Fortieth Street. The cemetery contains a large obelisk marking the grave of Maj. Gen. John B. Magruder, as well as the grave of famous fire-eater secessionist Lewis Trezevant Wigfall. Wigfall, a former Texas Confederate senator who served briefly as a Rebel officer, was said to have rowed out to Fort Sumter without authorization and demanded the surrender of Maj. Robert Anderson. Before the war, Anderson served as the inspector of ironworks in Trenton, New Jersey, where he inspected the iron elements that are still part of the exterior of Galveston's customhouse.

Perhaps the most poignant memorial for the Battle of Galveston stands in the center of Trinity Cemetery. A small tombstone with an anchor on top marks the grave of Lieut. Cmdr. Edward Lea, the first officer of the Union steamer *Harriet Lane*. Edward's father, Maj. Albert Lea, was serving on Magruder's staff during the battle—a father was literally fighting against his child. At the conclusion of the fighting, Albert Lea rushed over to find his son lying mortally wounded on the *Lane*'s deck. While Albert went away to try and secure medical help, Edward died. His last words, "My father is here," are inscribed on his small grave marker. A historical marker next to the grave describes the younger Lea's funeral service, which was attended by both Union and Confederate participants in the battle. Since Capt. J. M. Wainwright of the *Harriet Lane* had been a member of the Masonic order, the Galveston Masons volunteered to conduct their funeral rituals for him.

Account by Maj. Albert M. Lea of the Joint Funeral Service Conducted January 2, 1863, for Capt. J. M. Wainwright and Lieut. Cmdr. Edward Lea, USS *Harriet Lane*

It devolved upon me to say the burial service for the two deceased officers. I held the prayer book of my son in my hand, and penciling a few lines in the fly-leaf, showed them to General Magruder, who approved them. At the grave, the impressive Masonic services, as to the deceased Captain, had been joined in by the brethren of both nations. When the sublime office for the burial of the dead of the Episcopal Church was said by myself, for both laid in one grave, and then I added these words, as nearly as I can recall them: "My friends the wise men has said there is a time to rejoice and a time to mourn. Surely this is a time when we may weep with those that weep. Allow one so sorely tried, in this his willing sacrifice, to beseech you to believe that, whilst with strong arms and brave hearts we defend our rights, those we meet in battle may have brave and honest hearts as well as ourselves. Brave men are ever generous to the unfortunate. We have buried here two brave and honest gentlemen. Peace be to their ashes. Let us tread lightly o'er their graves. Amen." [Hayes, *Galveston*, 2:573]

Stop 5—Texas City Museum and USS *Westfield* Exhibit

One of the most interesting and least visited museum displays concerning the Battle of Galveston is at the Texas City Museum, located at 409 Sixth Street N., Texas City, TX 77592. Texas City is a small town located on the mainland about fourteen miles northwest of Galveston. When the US Army Corps of Engineers decided to expand the Texas City channel, it was necessary to salvage the wreck of USS *Westfield*. This was accomplished in 2009, when over eight thousand artifacts were recovered as part of the largest salvage operation ever conducted in Texas waters. The most important items were conserved at the Conservation Research Laboratory at Texas A&M University. They are now on display in the museum. One of the highlights of this exhibit is *Westfield*'s nine-inch Dahlgren cannon and the folding armor plates that this converted ferry-gunboat used in battle. A large portion of the vessel's boiler and steam machinery has been reconstructed. Because of the wide variety of artifacts, this is one of the finest Civil War gunboat exhibits in the country.

Report of Asst. Eng. W. S. Long, Department of the Gulf, United States Army, Concerning the Destruction of USS *Westfield* on the Morning of January 1, 1863

It was now about 8 o'clock. Captain Renshaw ordered the [transports] *Saxon* and *Mary Boardman* to come near the *Westfield* and take off her crew, as he intended to blow her up. The crew was all got off with the exception of Captain Renshaw, Lieutenant Zimmerman, two other officers, and the crew of the captain's gig, who remained until the last to fire the vessel. The fire was applied, Captain Renshaw was descending the ladder, and all the rest were in the boat, when (at 8:45) the after magazine prematurely exploded, and they were all blown up with the vessel. [Report of W. S. Long to D. C. Houston, New Orleans, LA, January 10, 1863, *ORN*, 19:460]

3. Battle of Sabine Pass

Driving from Galveston to Sabine Pass requires returning to Houston and then proceeding east on Interstate Highway 10 to reach Port Arthur. The distance is approximately 133 miles. The Sabine Pass Battleground and Historic Site is located at 6100 Dowling Road, Port Arthur, TX 77641. As this mailing address reflects, the small community of Sabine Pass is today incorporated as a part of Port Arthur. This site is situated at the southern tip of the border between Texas and Louisiana, where the Sabine River empties into the Gulf of Mexico. The battlefield, probably one of the least visited of all American Civil War battlefields, can be reached by traveling about thirteen miles south from Port Arthur on Texas Highway 87. The Sabine Pass Battleground is the closest thing that Texas has to a Civil War battlefield park, and a visit there is well worth the effort. Although small, the park does an outstanding job of interpreting the remarkable events of September 8, 1863. Visitors can see a number of monuments relating to both sides in the conflict, as well as many good interpretive panels.

One unique aspect of the Sabine Pass park is its excellent scale model showing the Confederate fort (Fort Griffin) and the ships that attacked it. The historic site also features a 1936 statue by artist Herring Coe depicting Dowling during the battle. At its base, the monument includes a list naming each of the officers and men that made up the fort's small garrison. When I give tours of the battlefield, I encourage visitors to stand at the Dowling monument and look across the water toward the lighthouse and the entrance to the pass. It was in this general location, with the Union fleet fully in view, that Dowling and his men made the critical decision discussed in this book (arguably the most critical decision in this book) to stay and fight. Much of the Confederate fort Dowling defended was destroyed by the subsequent widening of the channels in the pass, and the park today includes only a small part of the location of the western part of Fort Griffin. No trace of the stronghold remains visible today.

Report of Lieut. Richard W. Dowling, Company F, Cook's First Texas Heavy Artillery, Concerning the Battle of Sabine Pass

Thus it will be seen we captured with 47 men two gunboats, mounting thirteen guns of the heaviest caliber, and about 350 prisoners. All my men behaved like heroes; not a man flinched from his post. Our motto was "Victory or death." I beg leave to make particular mention of Private Michael McKernan, who, from his well-known capacity as gunner, I assigned as gunner to one of the guns, and nobly did he do his duty. It was his shot struck the *Sachem* in her steam drum. [Report of R. W. Dowling to F. H. Odlum, Fort Griffin, Sabine Pass, TX, September 9, 1863, *ORN*, 19:560]

One of the unique features of the Sabine Pass Battleground is that it includes the original "walking beam" of USS *Clifton*, one of the Union gunboats that attacked the Confederate position. This vessel was present at the Battle of Galveston and then was disabled and captured at the Battle of Sabine Pass. The battlefield also includes a historic marker relating to the capture of USS *Morning Light*. Visible across the pass on the Louisiana shore is the 1857 Sabine Pass lighthouse. Designed by engineer and later Confederate brigadier general Danville Leadbetter, this historic beacon was the site of repeated skirmishes between Union and Confederate forces. Now in the process of restoration, the lighthouse is a distinctive feature in contemporary depictions of the battle.

While visiting the Sabine Pass Battleground, the author encourages readers to visit the nearby Museum of the Gulf Coast, which is located at 700 Procter Street, Port Arthur, TX 77640. Occupying thirty-nine thousand square feet and two stories, the facility has an excellent collection of cultural materials. The Hall of Fame galleries highlight local musicians, athletes, and notables who have achieved national or international recognition such as Janis

Joplin, the Big Bopper, Jimmy Johnson, Karen Silkwood, actress Evelyn Keyes, and artist Robert Rauschenberg. Although only a few exhibits in the museum concern the Civil War, quite a few interesting maritime artifacts are on display, including the original Fresnel lens of the Sabine Banks light-house. I have taken many tour groups to this museum over the years as part of a Sabine Pass trip, and it consistently impresses visitors.

4. Miscellaneous Museum Collections

Two Austin museums with interesting Civil War exhibits are the Bullock Texas State History Museum at 1800 Congress Avenue, Austin, TX 78701, and the Texas Military Forces Museum at Camp Mabry, 3038 W. Thirty-Fifth Street, Austin, TX 78703. The US Army Medical Museum, which is located at 3898 Stanley Road, Building 1046, at Fort Sam Houston, San Antonio, TX, and the museum at Fort Sam Houston have excellent exhibits covering the army's operations over its long history (including the Civil War). U. S. Grant visited the historic Quadrangle at Fort Sam Houston in 1880.

One excellent facility that is off the beaten path is the Pearce Museum at Navarro College, located at 3100 Collin Street, Corsicana, TX 75110. It has a great collection of documents, artifacts, and photographs, many of which relate to the Civil War. In Corpus Christi, the Britton-Evans Centennial House, at 411 North Upper Broadway Street, preserves its history as a Confederate hospital. The public library and the Corpus Christi Museum of Science and History, located 1900 N. Chaparral Street, also have Civil War exhibits. Other Texas museums with Civil War collections include the Texas Maritime Museum, at 1202 Navigation Circle, Rockport, TX, and Fort Brown and Historic Brownsville Museum, at 1325 E. Washington Street, Brownville, TX.

Houston has at least two museums that will be of interest to Civil War aficionados. The former Museum of Southern History is now housed on the campus of Houston Christian University at the Morris Cultural Arts Center, 7502 Fondren Road, Houston, TX 77074. Its Civil War displays include weapons, documents, and artifacts such as a bell attributed to USS *Harriet Lane*. The Buffalo Soldiers National Museum, located at 3816 Caroline Street, Houston, TX 77004, has extensive exhibits relating to Black soldiers in the Civil War and the role their military descendants played afterward in the Indian Wars and the history of the Southwest.

5. Union Monument

Like many southern states, Texas has numerous monuments to Confederate soldiers in its cemeteries and courthouse squares. But the oldest Civil War memorial in Texas (dedicated in 1866) is the Treue Der Union Monument located on High Street in the small town of Comfort. This striking limestone obelisk is inscribed with the names of thirty-six men killed as a result of the Battle of the Nueces, which took place in Kinney County on August 10, 1862. These men were Union sympathizers, primarily German immigrants, who were killed while trying to make their way to Mexico to avoid Confederate service.

6. Cemeteries

Although there are many cemeteries with interesting monuments for Civil War figures, the Texas State Cemetery at 909 Navasota Street in Austin is particularly notable. Its southeast section, known as the Confederate Fields, contains the graves of more than 2,200 Confederate veterans and their wives. The burials include Gen. Albert Sidney Johnston, whose metal Gothic-style tomb and white marble recumbent statue were designed and carved by noted sculptor Elisabet Ney in 1902 (for more, visit https://www.battlefields.org /learn/biographies/albert-sidney-johnston). Along with Johnston, other Civil War notables buried in the cemetery include Brig. Gens. William Polk Hardeman, Adam Rankin "Stovepipe" Johnson, Ben McCulloch, William Read Scurry, and Maj. Gen. John Austin Wharton (for additional informa-tion, see https://www.battlefields.org/learn/biographies/benjamin-mcculloch and https://www.battlefields.org/learn/biographies/william-r-scurry). Several members of Dick Dowling's Davis Guard are also buried here. Confederate general Thomas Green is buried not far away in Oakwood Cemetery, located at 1601 Navasota Street.

7. Houses and Plantations

Texas boasts many preserved historic houses with connections to the Civil War. One of the most interesting is the Sam Bell Maxey House, located at 812 Church Street in Paris, TX, which has the distinction of being a state historic site. Maxey was a two-term US senator who served as a major general in the Confederate army. Located in downtown Houston at 1100 Bagby, the Heri-tage Society at Sam Houston Park is a museum complex that includes a num-ber of important historic structures. One is the 1850 Nichols-Rice-Cherry House. During the Civil War, Ebenezar Nichols served as finance com-missioner for Texas while it was preparing to join the Confederacy. He also served on General Magruder's staff during the Battle of Galveston. Nichols's office building, which was one of the first headquarters for Confederate forces in Texas, still stands in Galveston at 2021–23 Strand.

In addition to historic houses, two historic plantations in Texas are worth visiting. One is the Varner-Hogg Plantation, which is maintained by the Texas Historical Commission. Located at 1702 N. Thirteenth Street in West Columbia, TX, the plantation began with a grant of land in 1824 and changed uses many times during its long and impressive history. The site is particularly interesting for its interpretation of African American history and the legacy of the large number of enslaved people who lived and worked there. Also maintained by the Texas Historical Commission, the Levi Jordan Plantation State Historic Site, located at 10510 FM 524, Brazoria, TX 77422, preserves history from the state's antebellum period through the Civil War and the later chaos of Reconstruction. The Juneteenth Order issued at Galveston in 1865 had an enormous impact in securing emancipation for the people who had been enslaved at plantations like Varner-Hogg and Levi Jordan.

8. Prison Sites

Camp Ford at Tyler was the largest Confederate prison camp west of the Mississippi River. Established in 1863, it was not closed until May 19, 1865. At its peak, the prison housed more than five thousand Union captives. A historic marker may be viewed at the Camp Ford Historic Park, located at 6500 US 271, Tyler, TX 75708. Camp Groce, another prison located near Hempstead, was started in the summer of 1863 and housed Union prisoners from the Battles of Galveston and Sabine Pass. Camp Groce is the subject of a memorial at the Union Army P.O.W. Cemetery Park, three miles west of Hempstead on the Austin Branch Road. In 1987 Waller County and the State of Texas officially recognized the site as one of the burial grounds of Union prisoners of war from Camp Groce.

APPENDIX II

UNION ORDER OF BATTLE

Battle of Galveston (January 1, 1863)

UNITED STATES NAVY
Texas Blockading Force, West Gulf Blockading Squadron
   Cmdre. William B. Renshaw
      USS *Westfield* (flagship), Cmdr. William B. Renshaw
      USS *Harriet Lane*, Cmdr. J. M. Wainwright
      USS *Clifton*, Lieut. Cmdr. Richard L. Law
      USS *Owasco*, Lieut. Cmdr. Henry Wilson
      USS *Sachem*, Act. Master Amos Johnson
      US Schooner *Corypheus*, Act. Master A. T. Spear

UNITED STATES ARMY
42nd Massachusetts Infantry
   Col. Isaac S. Burrell

Battle between Alabama and Hatteras off Galveston (January 11, 1863)

UNITED STATES NAVY
USS *Hatteras*
   Lieut. Cmdr. Homer C. Blake

Capture of the Morning Light *off Sabine Pass*
(January 21, 1863)

UNITED STATES NAVY
USS *Morning Light*
  Act. Master John Dillingham
US Schooner *Velocity*
  Act. Vol. Lieut. Nathan W. Hammond

Battle of Sabine Pass (September 8, 1863)

UNITED STATES NAVY
West Gulf Blockading Squadron, Texas Expedition
  Act. Vol. Lieut. Frederick Crocker
      USS *Clifton*, Act. Vol. Lieut. Frederick Crocker
      USS *Sachem*, Act. Vol. Lieut. Amos Johnson
      USS *Arizona*, Act. Master Howard Tibbits
      USS *Granite City*, Act. Master Charles W. Lamson
UNITED STATES ARMY
19th Army Corps
  Maj. Gen. William B. Franklin
1st Division
  Brig. Gen. Godfrey Weitzel
UNITED STATES ARMY SHARPSHOOTERS
  ON NAVAL VESSELS
75th New York Infantry (*Clifton*)
  Col. Henry B. Fitch
161st New York Volunteers (*Sachem*)
  Col. William B. Kinsey

APPENDIX III

CONFEDERATE ORDER OF BATTLE

Battle of Galveston (January 1, 1863)

CONFEDERATE NAVAL FORCES [Texas Marine Department]
Texas Marine Department
    Cmdre. Leon Smith
CSS *Bayou City (flagship)*
    Maj. Leon Smith
CSS *Neptune* No. 2
    Capt. William H. Sangster
Tender John F. Carr
    Capt. John Y. Lawless
Tender Lucy Gwinn
    Capt. John H. Sterrett

ARTILLERY ON CONFEDERATE STEAMERS
Cook's 1st Texas Heavy Artillery, Company B
    Capt. Armand R. Wier

CONFEDERATE STATES ARMY
Department of Texas, New Mexico, and Arizona
    Maj. Gen. John B. Magruder
Land Forces at the Battle of Galveston
    Brig. Gen. William R. Scurry

20th Texas Infantry
　　Lieut. Col. Leonard A. Abercrombie
21st Texas Infantry Battalion
　　Lieut. Col. William A. Griffin

SIBLEY'S BRIGADE
　　Col. Thomas Green
2nd Texas Cavalry
　　Col. Charles L. Pyron
4th Texas Cavalry
　　Brig. Gen. William R. Scurry
5th Texas Cavalry
　　Col. Thomas Green
7th Texas Cavalry
　　Lieut. Col. Arthur P. Bagby

ARTILLERY
Cook's 1st Texas Heavy Artillery
　　Col. Joseph J. Cook
7th Texas Artillery Battalion
　　Maj. Sidney T. Fontaine

STORMING PARTY AGAINST KUHN'S WHARF
　　Col. Joseph J. Cook

SHARPSHOOTERS ON THE CONFEDERATE STEAMERS
　　Col. Thomas Green

*Battle between **Alabama** and **Hatteras** off Galveston*
(January 11, 1863)

CONFEDERATE STATES NAVY
CSS *Alabama*
　　Capt. Raphael Semmes

*Capture of the **Morning Light** off Sabine Pass*
(January 21, 1863)

CONFEDERATE STATES ARMY
Sabine Pass Expedition
　　Maj. Oscar M. Watkins
11th Texas Infantry Battalion
　　Lieut. Col. Ashley Spaight

2nd Texas Cavalry
  Capt. Matthew Nolan

CONFEDERATE STATES ARTILLERY
Cook's 1st Texas Heavy Artillery, Company F
  Capt. Frederick H. Odlum

CONFEDERATE NAVAL FORCES [Texas Marine Department]
CSS *Josiah H. Bell*
  Capt. Charles Fowler (fleet commander)
CSS *Uncle Ben*
  Capt. William Johnson

Battle of Sabine Pass (September 8, 1863)

CONFEDERATE STATES ARMY (Garrison of Fort Griffin)
Cook's 1st Texas Heavy Artillery, Company F
  Lieut. Richard W. Dowling

NOTES

Preface

1. Edward T. Cotham Jr., *Battle on the Bay: The Civil War Struggle for Galveston* (Austin: University of Texas Press, 1998), 100–102.

2. Steven E. Woodworth, *Jefferson Davis and His Generals: The Failure of Confederate Command in the West* (Lawrence: University Press of Kansas, 1990), 125–62.

3. Stephen W. Sears, *To the Gates of Richmond: The Peninsula Campaign* (New York: Ticknor and Fields, 1992), 179–308; Stephen W. Sears, *Landscape Turned Red: The Battle of Antietam* (New York: Ticknor and Fields, 1983), 296–308.

4. Terrence J. Winschel, *Triumph and Defeat: The Vicksburg Campaign* (Mason City, IA: Savas, 1999), 5–6, 177–84.

5. Alwyn Barr, "Texas Coastal Defense, 1861–1865," in *Lone Star Blue and Gray: Essays on Texas and the Civil War,* ed. Ralph A. Wooster and Robert Wooster, 2nd ed. (Austin: Texas State Historical Association, 2015), 187–88.

6. Earl Wesley Fornell, *The Galveston Era: The Texas Crescent on the Eve of Secession* (Austin: University of Texas Press, 1961), 5–6.

7. "Second Report of Conference for the Consideration of Measures for Effectually Blockading the Coast Bordering on the Gulf of Mexico,

Washington, D.C., Sept. 3, 1861," in US Naval War Records Office, *Official Records of the Union and Confederate Navies in the War of the Rebellion* (1905; repr., Harrisburg, PA: National Historical Society, 1987), 19:654. Hereafter, *Official Records of the Union and Confederate Navies* will be cited as *ORN* with all references being to series 1 unless otherwise indicated.

8. Fornell, *Galveston Era*, 23–24.

9. Willard Richardson, *The Texas Almanac for 1861* (Galveston, TX: Richardson, 1860), 236.

10. Andrew W. Hall, *The Galveston-Houston Packet: Steamboats on Buffalo Bayou* (Charleston, SC: History Press, 2012), 15, 89; Andrew Forest Muir, "Railroads Come to Houston, 1857–1861," *Southwest Historical Quarterly* 64, no. 1 (July 1960): 51–53.

11. Hall, *Galveston-Houston Packet*, 15, 89; Muir, "Railroads Come to Houston," 51-53.

Chapter 1

1. Cotham, *Battle on the Bay*, 17.

2. William C. Davis and Julie Hoffman, eds., *The Confederate General* (Harrisburg, PA: National Historical Society), 6:71; Cotham, *Battle on the Bay*, 27–28.

3. Sidney Sherman to "The Volunteer Troops of the City and County of Galveston," undated newspaper article in the Sherman Family Scrapbook, Sidney Sherman Papers, Rosenberg Library, Galveston, TX.

4. Cotham, *Battle on the Bay*, 37.

5. P. O. Hébert to Sec. of War, Galveston, September 27, 1861, *The War of the Rebellion: A Compilation of the Official Records of the Union and Confederate Armies*, series 1 (Washington, DC: Government Printing Office, 1896) 4:110. Hereafter, the *Official Records* will be cited as *OR* with all references being to series 1 unless otherwise indicated.

6. P. O. Hébert to J. P. Benjamin, Galveston, TX, November 15, 1861, *OR*, 4:139.

7. Cotham, *Battle on the Bay*, 42–49.

8. P. O. Hébert to J. P. Benjamin, Galveston, TX, October 31, 1861, *OR*, 4:131.

9. Hébert to Benjamin, Galveston, TX, November 15, 1861, *OR*, 4:139.

10. Hébert to Benjamin, Galveston, TX, November 15, 1861, *OR*, 4:139.

11. Cotham, *Battle on the Bay*, 52–53.

12. Francis Richard Lubbock, *Six Decades in Texas; or, Memoirs of Francis Richard Lubbock*, ed. C. W. Raines (Austin, TX: Ben C. Jones, 1900), 346–48.

13. Lubbock, *Six Decades in Texas*, 347–48.

14. Thomas North, *Five Years in Texas; or, What You Did Not Hear during the War from January 1861 to January 1866* (Cincinnati, OH: Elm Street Printing, 1871), 105–6.

15. P. O. Hébert to J. Deshler, San Antonio, TX, October 15, 1862, *OR*, 4:147.

16. Cotham, *Battle on the Bay*, 63–65.

17. Edward T. Cotham Jr., *The Southern Journey of a Civil War Marine* (Austin: University of Texas Press, 2006), 106–7.

18. D. G. Farragut to W. B. Renshaw, Pensacola Bay, FL, October 14, 1862, *ORN*, 19:260; D. G. Farragut to G. Welles, Pensacola Bay, FL, October 15, 1862, *ORN*, 19:253–54.

Chapter 2

1. Robert K. Krick, entry on John Bankhead Magruder, in *The Confederate General*, eds. William C. Davis and Julie Hoffman (Harrisburg, PA: National Historical Society, 1991), 4:139; Cotham, *Battle on the Bay*, 90–93.

2. Cotham, *Battle on the Bay*, 93–94.

3. Cotham, *Battle on the Bay*, 95–97; Daniel H. Hill, "McClellan's Change of Base and Malvern Hill," in *Battles and Leaders of the Civil War, Grant-Lee Edition* (1887; repr., Harrisburg, PA: Archive Society, 1991), vol. 2, pt. 2, p. 394.

4. Cotham, *Battle on the Bay*, 96–97.

5. Thomas M. Settles, *John Bankhead Magruder: A Military Reappraisal* (Baton Rouge: Louisiana State University Press, 2009), 185–86, 232.

6. Ezra J. Warner, *Generals in Gray: Lives of the Confederate Commanders* (Baton Rouge: Louisiana State University Press, 1959), 49; Settles, *Magruder*, 208–10, 215–16, 221–22, 230–31; Cotham, *Battle on the Bay*, 95.

7. Settles, *Magruder*, 232.

8. Settles, *Magruder*, 232–33.

9. Settles, *Magruder*, 139–42.

10. Gary W. Gallagher, *Lee and His Generals in War and Memory* (Baton Rouge: Louisiana State University Press, 1998), 135–36.

11. Settles, *Magruder*, 234–39.

12. "Special Orders No. 237," October 10, 1862, *OR*, 15:826; Settles, *Magruder*, 241.

13. John S. Ford, *RIP Ford's Texas*, ed. Stephen B. Oates (Austin: University of Texas Press, 1987), 343.

14. J. Magruder to E. Smith, Beaumont, TX, September 26, 1863, *OR* [Part 2], 26:261.

15. Cotham, *Battle on the Bay*, 107.

16. Lubbock, *Six Decades in Texas*, 424.

17. Cotham, *Battle on the Bay*, 107; Thomas M. Settles, "The Military Career of John Bankhead Magruder" (PhD diss., Texas Christian University, 1972), 238.

18. Charles P. Bosson, *History of the Forty-Second Regiment Infantry, Massachusetts Volunteers* (Boston: Mills, Knight, 1886), 67, 72.

19. Bosson, *History of the Forty-Second Regiment*, 74.

20. Charles W. Hayes, *Galveston: History of the Island and the City* (Austin, TX: Jenkins Garrett, 1974), 2:549; C. G. Forshey to J. B. Magruder, Rutersville, TX, December 2, 1862, *OR*, 15:885; Marjorie Waterfield, *Errant Rebel: The Life of Caleb G. Forshey* (Maumee, OH: no publisher, 2003), 93–98.

21. Report of J. B. Magruder, Galveston, TX, February 26, 1863, *OR*, 15:212.

22. US Naval War Records Office, *Officers in the Confederate States Navy, 1861–1865* (Washington, DC: Government Printing Office, 1898), 67.

23. W. W. Hunter to C. M. Mason, off San Jacinto, TX, September 14, 1862, *ORN*, 19:788.

24. Report of J. B. Magruder to S. Cooper, Galveston, TX, February 26, 1863, *OR*, 15:212.

25. Hayes, *Galveston*, 2:550.

26. Report of J. B. Magruder to S. Cooper, Galveston, TX, February 26, 1863, *OR*, 15:212.

27. D. G. Farragut to W. B. Renshaw, New Orleans, LA, December 12, 1862, *ORN*, 19:404.

28. Farragut to Renshaw, New Orleans, LA, December 12, 1862, *ORN*, 19:404.

29. Farragut to Renshaw, New Orleans, LA, December 12, 1862, *ORN*, 19:404.

30. Edward T. Cotham Jr., "Nothing but Disaster: The Failure of Union Plans to Capture Texas," in *The Seventh Star of the Confederacy: Texas during the Civil War*, ed. Kenneth W. Howell (Denton: University of North Texas Press, 2009), 136.

31. W. B. Renshaw to D. G. Farragut, Galveston, TX, October 8, 1862, *ORN*, 19:255–59.

32. Bosson, *History of the Forty-Second Regiment*, 76–77.

33. Bosson, *History of the Forty-Second Regiment*, 77.

34. Settles, *Magruder*, 204.

35. Cotham, *Battle on the Bay*, 113–15.

36. A. J. H. Duganne, *Camps and Prisons: Twenty Months in the Department of the Gulf* (New York: J. P. Robens, 1865), 233; Cotham, *Battle on the Bay*, 128.

37. Cotham, *Battle on the Bay*, 84.

38. Cotham, *Battle on the Bay*, 116.

39. Cotham, *Battle on the Bay*, 116.

40. Cotham, *Battle on the Bay*, 116, 120–21.

41. Cotham, *Battle on the Bay*, 124.

42. Cotham, *Battle on the Bay*, 124; Hall, *Galveston-Houston Packet*, 75–76.

43. Hall, *Galveston-Houston Packet*, 70–71; Andrew W. Hall and James M. Schmidt, "Battle of Galveston," *Civil War Navy: The Magazine* vol. 5, no. 3 (Winter 2018): 11.

44. Robert M. Franklin, *Battle of Galveston: A Speech Delivered to the Magruder Camp of the United Confederate Veterans, Galveston, Texas, April 2, 1911* (facsimile reprint of the original pamphlet, Galveston: San Luis, 1975), 8.

45. Franklin, *Battle of Galveston*, 8; Hall, *Galveston-Houston Packet*, 76.

46. Franklin, *Battle of Galveston*, 8.

47. Franklin, *Battle of Galveston*, 9.

48. Report of J. B. Magruder, Galveston, TX, January 1, 1863, *OR*, 15:210.

49. Farragut to Renshaw, New Orleans, LA, *ORN*, 19:404.

50. Cotham, *Battle on the Bay*, 129.

51. Cotham, *Battle on the Bay*, 132–33.

52. Justin Parkoff, "'A Formidable Looking Pile of Iron Boilers and Machinery': Reconstructing the Civil War Gunboat USS *Westfield*" (PhD diss., Texas A&M University, 2016); Jessica Rose Stika, "The Conservation and Analysis of Small Artifacts from the Site of USS *Westfield*" (master's thesis, Texas A&M University, 2013); Amy Borgens and Robert Gearhart, "USS *Westfield*: The Loss and Rediscovery of a Civil War Ferry-Gunboat in Galveston Bay," *Current Archeology in Texas* 12, no. 2 (November 2010): 1–9.

Chapter 3

1. David H. Strother, *A Virginia Yankee in the Civil War: The Diaries of David Hunt Strother*, ed. Cecil B. Edby (Chapel Hill: University of North Carolina Press, 1961), 142.

2. Strother, *Virginia Yankee in the Civil War*, 142–43.

3. Spencer C. Tucker, "*Alabama*, CSS," in *Encyclopedia of the American Civil War*, eds. David S. Heidler and Jeanne T. Heidler (Santa Barbara, CA: ABC-CLIO, 2000), 1:58.

4. Tucker, "*Alabama*, CSS," in Heidler and Heidler, *Encyclopedia of the American Civil War*, 1:58; extracts from private diary of Cmdre. H. H. Bell, December 3–26, 1862, *ORN*, 19:734.

5. D. G. Farragut to Gideon Welles, New Orleans, LA, January 3, 1863, *ORN*, 19:437–38; D. G. Farragut to Gideon Welles, New Orleans, LA, January 29, 1863, *ORN*, 19:440.

6. Gideon Welles, entry for January 28, 1863, in *The Civil War Diary of Gideon Welles: Lincoln's Secretary of the Navy*, eds. William E. Gienapp and Erica L. Gienapp (Urbana: University of Illinois Press, 2014), 131.

7. Loyall Farragut, *The Life of David Glasgow Farragut: First Admiral of the United States Navy* (New York: D. Appleton, 1879), 304–5.

8. Farragut, *Life of David Glasgow Farragut*, 304.

9. Farragut, *Life of David Glasgow Farragut*, 305.

10. Edward T. Cotham Jr., *Sabine Pass: The Confederacy's Thermopylae* (Austin: University of Texas Press, 2004), 21.

11. Farragut, *Life of David Glasgow Farragut*, 306.

12. Extracts from private diary of Cmdre. H. H. Bell, January 3, 1863, *ORN*, 19:735; D. G. Farragut to H. H. Bell, New Orleans, LA, January 3, 1863, *ORN*, 19:479.

13. Extracts from private diary of Cmdre. H. H. Bell, January 9, 1863, *ORN*, 19:736.

14. Extracts from private diary of Cmdre. H. H. Bell, January 10, 1863, *ORN*, 19:736.

15. Extracts from private diary of Cmdre. H. H. Bell, January 11, 1863, *ORN*, 19:736–37; letter from Frederick H. Thompson, Galveston, TX, January 10, 1863, *ORN*, 19:505.

16. D. G. Farragut to H. H. Bell, New Orleans, LA, January 12, 1863, *ORN*, 19:511.

17. Extracts from private diary of Cmdre. H. H. Bell, January 12, 1863, *ORN*, 19:737–38.

18. Cotham, *Battle on the Bay*, 149.

19. Paul H. Silverstone, *Warships of the Civil War Navies* (Annapolis, MD: Naval Institute Press, 1989), 35.

20. Tucker, "*Alabama*, CSS," in Heidler and Heidler, *Encyclopedia of the American Civil War*, 1:22.

21. Andrew W. Hall and Edward T. Cotham Jr., "13 Minutes in the Gulf," *Civil War Monitor* (Spring 2013): 40–41.

22. Raphael Semmes, *Memoirs of Service Afloat during the War between the States* (Secaucus, NJ: Blue and Grey, 1987), 520.

23. "The Great Cruiser," *Constitution* (Atlanta), August 29, 1886, 7.

24. Tucker, "*Alabama*, CSS," in Heidler and Heidler, *Encyclopedia of the American Civil War*, 1:22; Semmes, *Memoirs of Service Afloat*, 520.

25. Semmes, *Memoirs of Service Afloat*, 541.

26. Semmes, *Memoirs of Service Afloat*, 541.

27. Semmes, *Memoirs of Service Afloat*, 542.

28. Semmes, *Memoirs of Service Afloat*, 542.

29. Hall and Cotham, "13 Minutes in the Gulf," 43–47.

30. D. G. Farragut to G. Welles, New Orleans, LA, January 15, 1863, *ORN*, 19:506.

31. Farragut to Welles, New Orleans, LA, January 15, 1863, *ORN*, 19:506; D. G. Farragut to G. Welles, New Orleans, LA, January 21, 1863, *ORN*, 19:552–53.

32. Farragut to Welles, New Orleans, LA, January 21, 1863, *ORN*, 19:552–53.

33. Cotham, *Sabine Pass*, 51–52.

34. Cotham, *Sabine Pass*, 53–56.

35. Farragut to Welles, New Orleans, LA, January 21, 1863, *ORN*, 19:552–53.

36. D. Farragut to H. Bell, New Orleans, LA, February 6, 1863, *ORN*, 19:603–4.

Chapter 4

1. Paul Brueske, *The Last Siege: The Mobile Campaign* (Philadelphia: Casemate, 2018), xv–xvi.

2. Brueske, *Last Siege*, xvi.

3. John C. Waugh, *Last Stand at Mobile* (Abilene, TX: McWhiney Foundation Press, 2001), 22; John S. Sledge, *These Rugged Days: Alabama in the Civil War* (Tuscaloosa: University of Alabama Press, 2017), 122–24; Robert C. Jones, *Alabama and the Civil War: A History and Guide* (Charleston, SC: History Press, 2017), 6, 131, 144–45; Brueske, *Last Siege*, xvi–xvii.

4. Cotham, "Nothing but Disaster," 136: Waugh, *Last Stand at Mobile*, 15.

5. Waugh, *Last Stand at Mobile*, 19–20.

6. Waugh, *Last Stand at Mobile*, 18.

7. Cotham, *Battle on the Bay*, 51; Cotham, "Nothing but Disaster," 136; Cotham, *Sabine Pass*, 84.

8. Edward Shawcross, *The Last Emperor of Mexico* (New York: Basic Books, 2021), 83–85.

9. Shawcross, *Last Emperor of Mexico*, 75.

10. Stephen A. Dupree, *Planting the Union Flag in Texas: The Campaigns of Major General Nathaniel P. Banks in the West* (College Station: Texas A&M University Press, 2008), 4–7.

11. Carland Elaine Crook, "Benjamin Théron and French Designs in Texas during the Civil War," *Southwestern Historical Quarterly* vol. 68, no. 4 (April 1965): 435–43.

12. A. Lincoln to U. S. Grant, Washington, DC, August 9, 1863, in Abraham Lincoln, *Collected Works of Abraham Lincoln*, eds. Roy P. Basler, Maria D. Pratt, and Lloyd A. Dunlap (Springfield, IL: Abraham Lincoln Association, 1953), 6:374.

13. Edward T. Cotham Jr., *Juneteenth: The Story behind the Celebration* (Schreiner, TX: State House Press, 2021), 161–62.

14. National Oceanic and Atmospheric Administration, "Shoreline Mileage of the United States," NOAA Office for Coastal Management,

accessed August 28, 2022, https://coast.noaa.gov/data/docs/states /shorelines.pdf.

15. Kurt Henry Hackemer, "Strategic Dilemma: Civil-Military Friction and the Texas Coastal Campaign of 1863," *Military History of the West* vol. 26, no. 2 (Fall 1996): 196–99.

16. Dupree, *Planting the Union Flag in Texas*, 16–21.

17. A. Lincoln to N. P. Banks, Washington, DC, August 5, 1863, in Abraham Lincoln, *Collected Works of Abraham Lincoln*, eds. Roy P. Basler, Maria D. Pratt, and Lloyd A. Dunlap (Springfield, IL: Abraham Lincoln Association, 1953), 6:364–65; H. W. Halleck to N. P. Banks, Washington, DC, August 6, 1863, *OR* [Part 1], 26:672.

18. H. W. Halleck to N. P. Banks, Washington, DC, August 10, 1863, *OR* [Part 1], 26:673.

19. H. W. Halleck to N. P. Banks, Washington, DC., August 28, 1863, *OR* [Part 1], 26:699.

20. Cotham, *Sabine Pass*, 85; Welles, *Diary of Gideon Welles*, 1:391.

21. Brownson Malsch, "Indianola, TX," *Handbook of Texas Online*, accessed August 29, 2022, https://www.tshaonline.org/handbook/entries /indianola-tx.

22. Cotham, *Southern Journey of a Civil War Marine*, 114–15.

23. N. P. Banks to H. W. Halleck, New Orleans, LA, August 26, 1863, *OR* [Part 1], 26:697.

24. N. P. Banks to H. W. Halleck, New Orleans, LA, August 15, 1863, *OR* [Part 1], 26:683.

25. Banks to Halleck, New Orleans, LA, August 26, 1863, *OR* [Part 1], 26:696.

26. Banks to Halleck, New Orleans, LA, August 26, 1863, *OR* [Part 1], 26:696.

27. N. P. Banks to H. W. Halleck, New Orleans, LA, October 22, 1863, *OR* [Part 1], 26:308.

28. Cotham, *Sabine Pass*, 15–16, 28–30.

29. J. Kellersberg to X. B. Debray, Harrisburg, TX, July 30, 1862, *OR*, 9:729; Cotham, *Sabine Pass*, 69.

30. Cotham, *Sabine Pass*, 69–71.

31. Cotham, *Sabine Pass*, 76–77.

32. Cotham, *Sabine Pass*, 71–76.

33. Cotham, *Sabine Pass*, 71–77.

34. Cotham, *Sabine Pass*, 94.

35. Cotham, *Sabine Pass*, 28–31, 93–94.

36. Cotham, *Sabine Pass*, 101–2.

37. Cotham, *Sabine Pass*, 99.

38. H. H. Bell to G. Welles, New Orleans, LA, September 4, 1863, *ORN*, 20:515.

39. Cotham, *Sabine Pass*, 132–35.

40. Cotham, *Sabine Pass*, 135–41.

41. Cotham, *Sabine Pass*, 117, 205.

42. Cotham, *Sabine Pass*, 118–20, 135.

43. Cotham, *Sabine Pass*, 79–81, 119–21, 148.

44. Cotham, *Sabine Pass*, 121–23.

45. Cotham, *Sabine Pass*, 129, 141.

46. Cotham, *Sabine Pass*, 147–48, 159.

47. Report of R. W. Dowling to F. H. Odlum, Sabine Pass, TX, September 9, 1863, *ORN*, 20:559–60.

48. Cotham, *Sabine Pass*, 125–26.

49. Cotham, *Sabine Pass*, 113–14, 148–54.

50. Cotham, *Sabine Pass*, 140, 148–50.

51. Cotham, *Sabine Pass*, 115.

52. Cotham, *Sabine Pass*, 149–53.

53. Cotham, *Sabine Pass*, 149–56.

Chapter 5

1. N. P. Banks to A. Lincoln, New Orleans, LA, October 22, 1863, *OR* [Part 1] 26:290–92.

2. Dupree, *Planting the Union Flag in Texas*, 11–13.

3. Madeleine Martin, "Niblett's Bluff," *Handbook of Texas Online*, accessed October 1, 2022, https://www.tshaonline.org/handbook/entries/nibletts-bluff.

4. Richard Lowe, *The Texas Overland Expedition of 1863* (Fort Worth, TX: Ryan Place, 1996), 31–34.

5. Lowe, *Texas Overland Expedition of 1863*, 36–39.

6. Lowe, *Texas Overland Expedition of 1863*, 27–29.

7. Lowe, *Texas Overland Expedition of 1863*, 26.

8. Stephen A. Townsend, *The Yankee Invasion of Texas* (College Station, TX: Texas A&M University Press, 2006), 15; Dupree, *Planting the Union Flag in Texas*, 70.

9. Fred Harvey Harrington, *Fighting Politician: Major General Nathaniel P. Banks* (Westport, CT: Greenwood, 1948), 133, 140.

10. Dupree, *Planting the Union Flag in Texas*, 63–65; N. P. Banks to A. Lincoln, New Orleans, LA, October 22, 1863, *OR* [Part 1] 26:292.

11. Dupree, *Planting the Union flag in Texas*, 70–71.

12. Lowe, *Texas Overland Expedition of 1863*, 61.

13. Dupree, *Planting the Union flag in Texas*, 67–68; Lowe, *Texas Overland Expedition of 1863*, 80–100.

14. Lowe, *Texas Overland Expedition of 1863*, 61.

15. Bobby J. McKinney, *Confederates on the Caney: An Illustrated Account of the Civil War on the Texas Gulf Coast* (Rosenberg, TX: Mouth of Caney Publication, 1994), 1–2; Dupree, *Planting the Union flag in Texas*, 70–71, 77–79.

16. Townsend, *Yankee Invasion of Texas*, 70-71.

17. Cotham, *Juneteenth*, 165–67.

18. Dupree, *Planting the Union flag in Texas*, 79.

Chapter 6

1. Cotham, *Battle on the Bay*, 183; William C. Barnett, "A Tale of Two Cities: Houston, the Industrial Metropolis, and Galveston, the Island Getaway," in *Energy Metropolis: An Environmental History of Houston and the Gulf Coast*, eds. Martin V. Melosi and Joseph A. Pratt, (Pittsburgh: University of Pittsburgh Press, 2007), 186, 190–93.

2. Cotham, *Sabine Pass*, 170–171.

3. Cotham, *Sabine Pass*, 6.

BIBLIOGRAPHY

Barnett, William C. "A Tale of Two Cities: Houston, the Industrial Metropolis, and Galveston, the Island Getaway." In *Energy Metropolis: An Environmental History of Houston and the Gulf Coast*, edited by Martin V. Melosi and Joseph A. Pratt, 185–204. Pittsburgh: University of Pittsburgh Press, 2007.

Barr, Alwyn. "Texas Coastal Defense, 1861–1865." In *Lone Star Blue and Gray: Essays on Texas and the Civil War*, edited by Ralph A. Wooster and Robert Wooster, 152-174. 2nd ed. Austin: Texas State Historical Association, 2015.

Borgens, Amy, and Robert Gearhart. "USS *Westfield*: The Loss and Rediscovery of a Civil War Ferry-Gunboat in Galveston Bay." *Current Archeology in Texas* 12, no. 2 (November 2010): 1–9.

Bosson, Charles P. *History of the Forty-Second Regiment Infantry, Massachusetts Volunteers*. Boston: Mills, Knight, 1886.

Brueske, Paul. *The Last Siege: The Mobile Campaign*. Philadelphia: Casemate, 2018.

Cotham, Edward T., Jr. *Battle on the Bay: The Civil War Struggle for Galveston*. Austin: University of Texas Press, 1998.

———. *Juneteenth: The Story behind the Celebration*. Kerrville, TX: State House Press, 2021.

———. "Nothing but Disaster: The Failure of Union Plans to Capture Texas." In *The Seventh Star of the Confederacy: Texas during the Civil War*, edited by Kenneth W. Howell, 130–148. Denton: University of North Tex as Press, 2009.

———. *Sabine Pass: The Confederacy's Thermopylae*. Austin: University of Texas Press, 2004.

———. *The Southern Journey of a Civil War Marine: The Illustrated Notebook of Henry O. Gusley*. Austin: University of Texas Press, 2006.

Crook, Carland Elaine. "Benjamin Théron and French Designs in Texas during the Civil War." *Southwestern Historical Quarterly* 68, no. 4 (April 1965): 432–54.

Davis, William C., and Julie Hoffman, eds. *The Confederate General*. 6 vols. Harrisburg, PA: National Historical Society, 1991.

Duganne, A. J. H. *Camps and Prisons: Twenty Months in the Department of the Gulf*. New York: J. P. Robens, 1865.

Dupree, Stephen A. *Planting the Union Flag in Texas: The Campaigns of Major General Nathaniel P. Banks in the West*. College Station: Texas A&M University Press, 2008.

Farragut, Loyall. *The Life of David Glasgow Farragut: First Admiral of the United States Navy*. New York: D. Appleton, 1879.

Ford, John S. *RIP Ford's Texas*. Edited by Stephen B. Oates. Austin: University of Texas Press, 1987.

Fornell, Earl Wesley. *The Galveston Era: The Texas Crescent on the Eve of Secession*. Austin: University of Texas Press, 1961.

Franklin, Robert M. *Battle of Galveston: A Speech Delivered to the Magruder Camp of the United Confederate Veterans, Galveston, Texas, April 2, 1911*. Facsimile reprint of the original pamphlet. Galveston: San Luis, 1975.

Frazier, Donald S. *Cottonclads: The Battle of Galveston and the Defense of the Texas Coast*. Fort Worth, TX: Ryan Place, 1996.

Gallagher, Gary W. *Lee and His Generals in War and Memory*. Baton Rouge: Louisiana State University Press, 1998.

Hackemer, Kurt Henry. "Strategic Dilemma: Civil-Military Friction and the Texas Coastal Campaign of 1863." *Military History of the West* 26, no. 2 (Fall 1996): 187–214.

Hall, Andrew W. *The Galveston-Houston Packet: Steamboats on Buffalo Bayou*. Charleston, SC: History Press, 2012.

Hall, Andrew W., and Edward T. Cotham Jr. "13 Minutes in the Gulf." *Civil War Monitor* (Spring 2013): 39–49.

Hall, Andrew W., and James M. Schmidt. "Battle of Galveston." *Civil War Navy: The Magazine* 5, no. 3 (Winter 2018): 4–13.

Harrington, Fred Harvey. *Fighting Politician: Major General Nathaniel P. Banks.* Westport, CT: Greenwood, 1948.

Hayes, Charles W. *Galveston: History of the Island and the City.* 2 vols. Austin, TX: Jenkins Garrett Press, 1974.

Heidler, David S., and Jeanne T. Heidler, eds. *Encyclopedia of the American Civil War.* 5 vols. Santa Barbara, CA: ABC-CLIO, 2000.

Jones, Robert C. *Alabama and the Civil War: A History and Guide.* Charleston, SC: History Press, 2017.

Kell, John McIntosh. "The Great Cruiser." *Constitution* (Atlanta), August 29, 1886, 7.

Lincoln, Abraham. *The Collected Works of Abraham Lincoln, 1809–1865.* Edited by Roy P. Basler, Maria D. Pratt, and Lloyd A. Dunlap. 9 vols. Springfield, IL: Abraham Lincoln Association, 1953.

Lowe, Richard. *The Texas Overland Expedition of 1863.* Fort Worth, TX: Ryan Place, 1996.

Lubbock, Francis Richard. *Six Decades in Texas; or, Memoirs of Francis Richard Lubbock, Governor of Texas in War Time, a Personal Experience in Business, War, and Politics.* Edited by C. W. Raines. Austin, TX: Ben C. Jones, 1900.

McKinney, Bobby J. *Confederates on the Caney: An Illustrated Account of the Civil War on the Texas Gulf Coast.* Rosenberg, TX: Mouth of Caney, 1994.

Muir, Andrew Forest. "Railroads Come to Houston, 1857–1861." *Southwest Historical Quarterly* 64, no. 1 (July 1960): 42–63.

National Oceanic and Atmospheric Administration. "Shoreline Mileage of the United States." NOAA Office for Coastal Management. Accessed August 28, 2022. https://coast.noaa.gov/data/docs/states/shorelines.pdf.

Parkoff, Justin. "'A Formidable Looking Pile of Iron Boilers and Machinery': Reconstructing the Civil War Gunboat USS *Westfield*." PhD diss., Texas A&M University, 2016.

Richardson, Willard. *The Texas Almanac for 1861.* Galveston, TX: Richardson, 1860.

Sears, Stephen W. *To the Gates of Richmond: The Peninsula Campaign.* New York: Ticknor and Fields, 1992.

———. *Landscape Turned Red: The Battle of Antietam.* New York: Ticknor and Fields, 1983.

Semmes, Raphael. *Memoirs of Service Afloat during the War between the States.* Secaucus, NJ: Blue and Grey, 1987.

Settles, Thomas M. *John Bankhead Magruder: A Military Reappraisal.* Baton Rouge: Louisiana State University Press, 2009.

———. "The Military Career of John Bankhead Magruder" PhD diss., Texas Christian University, 1972.

Shawcross, Edward. *The Last Emperor of Mexico.* New York: Basic Books, 2021.

Silverstone, Paul H. *Warships of the Civil War Navies.* Annapolis, MD: Naval Institute Press, 1989.

Sledge, John S. *These Rugged Days: Alabama in the Civil War.* Tuscaloosa: University of Alabama Press, 2017.

Stika, Jessica Rose. "The Conservation and Analysis of Small Artifacts from the Site of USS *Westfield.*" Master's thesis, Texas A&M University, 2013.

Strother, David H. *A Virginia Yankee in the Civil War: The Diaries of David Hunt Strother.* Edited by Cecil B. Edby. Chapel Hill: University of North Carolina Press, 1961.

Texas State Historical Association. *Handbook of Texas Online.* Last accessed January 3, 2023. https://www.tshaonline.org.

Tsouras, Peter G., ed. *The Greenhill Dictionary of Military Quotations.* London: Greenhill Books, 2000.

Tucker, Spencer C., ed. *The Civil War Naval Encyclopedia.* 2 vols. Santa Barbara, CA: ABC-CLIO, 2011.

US Naval War Records Office. *Official Records of the Union and Confederate Navies in the War of the Rebellion.* 27 vols. Washington, DC: US Government Printing Office, 1894–1922.

———. *Officers in the Confederate States Navy, 1861–1865.* Washington, DC: Government Printing Office, 1898.

US War Department. *The War of the Rebellion: A Compilation of the Official Records of the Union and Confederate Armies.* 128 vols. Washington, DC: US Government Printing Office, 1880–1901.

Warner, Ezra J. *Generals in Blue: Lives of the Union Commanders*. Baton Rouge: Louisiana State University Press, 1964.

———. *Generals in Gray: Lives of the Confederate Commanders*. Baton Rouge: Louisiana State University Press, 1959.

Waterfield, Marjorie. *Errant Rebel: The Life of Caleb G. Forshey*. Maumee, OH: no publisher, 2003.

Waugh, John C. *Last Stand at Mobile*. Abilene, TX: McWhiney Foundation Press, 2001.

Welles, Gideon. *The Civil War Diary of Gideon Welles: Lincoln's Secretary of the Navy*. Edited by William E. Gienapp and Erica L. Gienapp. Urbana: University of Illinois Press, 2014.

Winschel, Terrence J. *Triumph and Defeat: The Vicksburg Campaign*. Mason City, IA: Savas, 1999.

Woodworth, Steven E. *Jefferson Davis and His Generals: The Failure of Confederate Command in the West*. Lawrence: University Press of Kansas, 1990.

INDEX

Numbers in **boldface** refer to illustrations

26; and Selma, Alabama, 77, 79; and Texans, 78–79; and Texas, 79, 135. *See also* Confederate army; Confederate navy; Mobile, Alabama

Confederate army: and ammunition, 102; and Army of the Mississippi, 1; and attack of Kuhn's Wharf, 48; and Battle of Galveston, 47–49; and Battle of Sabine Pass, 94, 100, 101, 102; and Caney River, 113; and capture of Galveston, 14–15; and capture of Massachusetts infantry, 55; and Chickahominy River, 19; and command of Trans-Mississippi, 20–21; and construction of fortifications, 62, 63, 64, 70, 71, 86; and control of Galveston, 17, 63; and Cook's First Texas Heavy Artillery, 32, 96; and defense of Galveston Island, 5, 7, 8–12, 63, 64, 70; and defense of Richmond, 20; and District of Texas, New Mexico and Arizona, 125; and District of the Trans-Mississippi, 20; and Eagle Grove, 42; and Fort Griffin, 92, 93, 96; and Fort Sabine, 94, 95; and Galveston Bay, 14, 63; and Galveston Island, 11; and gunboats, 102; Hispanic soldiers in, 122; and Holly Springs raid, 2; and Hood's Texas Brigade, 78; importance of railroads to, 77; and John Bankhead Magruder, 19, 20, 21–22, 28, 30, 107, 108, 109, 117; and Maj. Gen. Richard Taylor, 108, 109; and Paul Octave Hebert, 8, 9–10, 11, 12, 13; and recapture of Galveston, 1, 12, 26–28, 64; and Sabine Pass fort, 108, 116; and Sam Bell Maxey, 135; and Seven Days' Campaign, 1–2, 20; and Sibley's Brigade contingent, 27, 129; soldiers of, 11, 14, 27, 32, 40, 78, 98; and Texian Army, 7, 127; and Union steamer *South*

Carolina, 5; and Vicksburg, 38; and victory at Bayou Bourbeau, 111–12; and Walker's Texas Division, 78; and William W. Hunter, 33. *See also* Battle of Sabine Pass; Taylor, Maj. Gen. Richard

Confederate navy: and Battle of Galveston, 35, **50**, 52–53, 57, 58, 59, 60; and capture of USS *Harriet Lane*, **53**, 59, 60, 70; command of, 33–34, 35; and "cottonclad" boats, 33, 35, 44, 49–51, 53, 71, 72, 109; and CSS *Alabama*, 71; and defense of Galveston Island, 9–10, 28; and Galveston Bay, 68; and Galveston Harbor, 39, 52; gunboats of, 31, 33, 34, 35, 39, 43, 49–51, 52, 55, 65, 109; and Leon Smith, 34–35, 44, 49–52, 55; and raider *Alabama*, 65, 67; and raiding of shipping, 65–67; and ramming enemy's boats, 50–53; and recapture of Galveston, 63, 71–72; and Sabine Pass, 71–72; sailors of, 51, 67; and Selma, Alabama, 77; ships of, 5, 33, 34, 35, 44, 49, 51, 52, 53, 55, 67, 71, 72, 73; and steamer *Josiah H. Bell*, 73; and steamer *Uncle Ben* , 71, 73; and William W. Hunter, 33–34. *See also* Magruder, Maj. Gen. John Bankhead; *Royal Yacht*

Cook, Col. Joseph J., 15, 32, 48, 96

Cooper, Inspector General Samuel, 20, 23

Crocker, Act. Vol. Lieut. Frederick, 94–95, 96, 100, 101

CSS *Alabama*, 65, 67, 68, **69**, 69, 70. *See also* Confederate navy; Galveston, Texas

Custer, George Armstrong, 113

Dana, Maj. Gen. Napoleon Jackson, 110

Davis, Pres. Jefferson, **21**; and commander-in-chief position, 116; and Confederate States of America, 21;

Davis, Pres. Jefferson (*cont.*)
decision of, 23, 24, 115; and John
Bankhead Magruder, 18, 21–22, 23,
24, 115, 116, 117; and Mexican War,
21; options of, 22–23; as Secretary
of War, 85; and use of camels, 85;
and West Point, 18, 21
Dowling, Lieut. Richard "Dick", 96,
97, 97–100, 116, 118, 132. *See also*
Battle of Sabine Pass

Eagle, Capt. Henry, 12
Elissa (ship), 122
Ellis Island, 124
Emancipation Proclamation, 38

Farragut, Adm. David G., **39**; aggressiveness of, 60, 61; and Battle
of Galveston, 58, 59, 60, 61; and
blockade outside Galveston Bay,
37; and capture of New Orleans,
60; decision of, 38; expectations
of, 55, 56; and Galveston, Texas,
38, 59–60, 61, 72–73; and letters
to Renshaw, 15, 37; and letter to
Commodore Bell, 74; and loss of
ships, 74; and military operations,
77, 78, 116; and Mobile Bay, 60;
naval operations of, 38, 39–40,
61–62, 81; options of, 36–38, 60–61;
and Port Hudson, 61; and recapture
of Galveston, 61–62, 63, 64; and
reinforcement troops, 17, 37; and
Secretary Welles, 70; and West
Gulf Blockading Squadron, 60,
61, 93–94
Farragut, Loyall, 60–61
Florida, 70
Ford, Col. John S. "RIP", 24
Forshey, Maj. Caleb G., 31–32
Fort Hatteras, 9
Fort Hébert, 12, 13, 14, 40
Fort Sumter, 9, 130

France, 79, 80, 81, 82, 84, 85
Franklin, Maj. Gen. William B., 81, 95,
96, 100, 102, 104. *See also* Battle of
Sabine Pass; Louisiana

Galveston, Houston and Henderson
Railroad, 4
Galveston, Texas: and Army of the
Trans-Mississippi, 121; and Banks
Expedition, 66; and building of
fortifications, 91; capture of (1862),
12, 14–15, 17, 24, 27, 43, 128; city of,
2, 9, 10, 11, 12, 14, 15, 17, 24, 26, 27,
37, 38, 39, 40, 42, 54, 55, 61, 63, 64,
65, 68, 86, 105, 115; civilians in, 11,
12, 13–14; and Confederate army,
12, 14, 26, 39, 47, 55, 63, 64, 108, 118;
Confederate control of, 68, 105,
110, 115, 118; and CSS *Alabama*, 72,
116, 117; decisions about, 117–18; defenses of, 7, 8–14, 26, 72, 75; evacuation of, 11, 12, 14, **15**; exports from,
3, 5; fortifications at, 74, 86, 90; and
Galveston Bay, 34, 86, 107, 124; and
Galveston Harbor, 17, 24, 31, 37, 39,
47, 64; Grand Opera House of, 129;
and headquarters of Confederates,
135; and Hendley Row Building,
124, 125, 126, **126**; and immigration,
124; island location of, 2, 4, 8, 9,
10, 104, 118; and John Bankhead
Magruder, 26, 74; Kuhn's Wharf
in, **46**, 46–47, 124; loss of, 116; and
Maj. Gen. Nathaniel Banks, 84, 86,
93, 104, 106–7, 118; military school
in, 31; and naval movements, 116;
and Nia Cultural Center, 127; and
Old Galveston Square Building,
127; port of, 2, 3, 4, 8, 9, 10, 11, 26,
37, 115; and railroad bridge, 40, 42;
and railroads, 14, 24, 107; raising
Union flag in, 115, 119, 128, 129; and
Raphael Semmes, 68, 70; recap-

ture of, 1, 24, 26, 27–28, 30–32, 47,
55, 60, 61–64, 68, 70, 71, 94; and
Sabine Pass, 132–33; sea attacks
of, 106; strategic decisions about,
115, 116; and Texans, 11, 13–14, 28;
threats to, 81, 109; Trinity Episcopal Cemetery in, 130; Union
control of, 40, 47, 65, 66, 105, 128;
and Union forces, 11, 12, 14, 24, 26,
27, 47, 55–56, 66, 74, 82, 83, 87, 96,
102, 104, 105, 109, 112, 113, 128; and
Union ships, 67. *See also* Battle of
Galveston; United States Custom
House and Courthouse
Galveston Bay, 2, **3**, 4, 5, 12, **25**. *See also*
Bell, Cmdre. Henry Haywood;
Confederate army; Confederate
navy; Union navy
Galveston Island: and city of Galveston, 9, 11, 122; defense of, 8–11, 12,
70; and Eagle Grove fort, 14, 40;
evacuation of, 10–11; fortifications
at, **41**; and gunboats, 10; and railroads, 5, 10, 14, 40, 43; retreat from,
11; and Union forces, 18
General Rusk (ship), 34
Granger, Maj. Gen. Gordon, 105, 127
Grant, Maj. Gen. Ulysses S.: and
historic Quadrangle, 134; and military operations, 77, 78, 80, 81, 108,
112–13; and production of *Othello*,
18; supply depot of, 2; and Vicksburg, 2, 38; and visit to historic
home, 130; and "western Texas", 82
Green, Gen. Thomas, 108, 135
Griffin, Col. William H., 91–92
Gulf of Mexico: and commerce
raiding, 66–67; and Confederate
crew, 69; and "Island City", 2; and
map of Texas Coast, **4**; and Sabine
River, 132; and Union army, 9, 64
guns: and ammunition, 7, 29, 47; and
artillery batteries, 30, 31, 32, 47,

48, 95; on the *Brooklyn* (ship), 65;
calibers of, 8–9, 133; and Confederate forces, 31, 32, 33, 36, 43, 47,
52, 54, 55, 58, 70, 72, 89, 97–99, 100,
102, 124; and Cook's First Texas
Heavy Artillery, 32; and evacuation
of island, 12; and Fort Griffin, 92,
95, 96, 98, 99, 101, 102; and Fort
Morgan, 77; and Fort Sabine, 97;
and four-day truce period, 14; and
gunboats, 131, 133; and howitzers,
97, 99, 124; movement of, 43; and
naval forces, 17, 24, 26, 37, 43, 71,
73–74, 92, 94, 95–97; placement
of, 70, 125–26; and sharpshooters'
shotguns, 52; and Union forces, 26,
29, 42, 71, 73–74, 89, 94, 98, 99, 129;
and USS *Westfield's* Dahlgren gun,
57, 58; on warships, 30; of *Westfield*
and Harriet Lane, 70. *See also* Battle
of Galveston; Confederate navy;
Union navy
Gusley, Henry O., 128

Halleck, General-in-Chief Henry,
82–83, 84, 85, 86, 87, 94. *See also*
Union army
Hébert, Brig. Gen. Paul Octave, **8**; and
artillery batteries, 12; as colonel
in First Louisiana Artillery, 8;
decision of, 11–12, 13, 14; decisions
of, 15; and defense of Galveston
Island, 8–12, 13, 24, 26; and evacuation of island, 11, 12; as governor
of Louisiana, 8; and lack of men
and armament, 27; and letters to
Secretary Benjamin, 8–9, 10; and
Mexican War, 7, 10; options of,
10–11; as a politician, 10, 11; and
retreat from Galveston Island, 11,
43; and Texans, 12, 14, 23; and West
Point, 7, 9
Hill, Gen. D. H., 19

Texas, New Mexico, and Arizona, 23; and District of the Trans-Mississippi, 20, 21; engineers of, 92; and funeral service, 131; and Galveston, Texas, 36, 65, 72; and Galveston Harbor, 58; grave of, 130; headquarters of, 130; and lack of men and armament, 27; and letters to Cmdre. Bell, 63; and Malvern Hill assault, 19–20, 22, 30; and Mexican War, 18–19, 21, 30, 48; military career of, 21, 22–23, 27, 28, 29–30, 34; and naval forces, 30, 32–35, 73–74; New Year's Day victory of, 68; and New Year's Eve offensive, 32; options of, 26–28, 30–31, 33–34, 39–40, 47–48, 71–72; and Peninsula Campaign, 22; and rail-mounted artillery, 43; and railroad bridge, 43; and recapture of Galveston, 26–28, 30–32, 34, 71; report of, 23, 125–26; reputation of, 19, 21, 22, 27–28; and results of wading charge, 48, 49; ruses of, 19; and Sabine Pass, 71, 72, 73; and Seven Days' Campaign, 20, 22; and steamer *Josiah H. Bell*, 71, 73–74; and Texans, 27–28; and Texas, 23–24, 26, 27, 90; and Union blockade, 71, 73; and waterfront guns, 55; and West Point, 18, 21, 29–30

Maryland, 2

Massachusetts, 108

Maximilian, Archduke, 79, 80

McClellan, Maj. Gen. George, 1, 2, 19, 20

McKernan, Private Michael, 133

Mexican War, 7, 10, 18, 21, 30, 48

Mexico, 4, 79, 80, 82, 84, 85. *See also* Lincoln, President Abraham; Texas

Mississippi, 2, 38, 75, 78, 79, 95

Mississippi River, 2, 20, 38, 60, 61, 75. *See also* Texas

Missouri, 2

Mobile, Alabama, 40, 76–77, 78, 79, 80, 81. *See also* Union

Mobile Bay, 77–78

Monitor (ship), 33

Napoleon III, 79

Neptune No. 2 (ship), 49, 51, 52

New Jersey, 9, 130

New Mexico, 1, 23

New York, 9, 60, 66, 93, 108

New York Times, The, 79

Ney, Elisabet, 135

Nichols, Ebenezar, 135

North Carolina, 60

Odlum, Capt. Frederick, 97

Ohio River, 1

Othello (Shakespeare), 18

Palmito Ranch Battle, 121–22

Pennsylvania, 33, 108

Reconstruction, 136

Renshaw, Cmdre. William B., **36**; and Admiral Farragut, 59; and capture of Galveston, 14, 15; as Commodore of Union fleet, 36, 37, 38, 40, 42, 49, 54–57, 58; death of, 39, 46, 57, 117, 132; decisions of, 42–43, 45–46, 54, 57–58; and Farragut's decisions, 116; and fate of USS *Westfield*, 55–58; and Galveston Bay, 39, 40, 117; and Galveston Harbor, 65; options of, 42, 44, 55–56; and railroad bridge, 40, 42–43; report of, 15; and source of light, 44–46; and truce periods, 14, 54

Richmond, Virginia: army in, 24; as Confederate capital, 1, 7, 19; and Confederate officials, 7, 8, 19, 20, 115; and John Bankhead Magruder, 26, 31; Lee's retreat from, 2; and population, 76; and summer of 1862, 38; Tredegar Iron Works in, 77